Radical Love

Yale

UNIVERSITY PRESS

NEW HAVEN AND LONDON

Translated and Edited by Omid Safi

RADICAL LOVE

TEACHINGS FROM
THE ISLAMIC
MYSTICAL
TRADITION

Yale University Press books may be purchased in quantity for educational,
business, or promotional use. For information, please e-mail
sales.press@yale.edu (U.S. office) or sales@yaleup.co.uk (U.K. office).

Designed by Nancy Ovedovitz and set in Garamond and Herculanum types
by Integrated Publishing Solutions.

Library of Congress Control Number: 2017952563

ISBN 978-0-300-22581-5 (hardcover : alk. paper)
ISBN 978-0-300-24861-6 (paperback)

A catalogue record for this book is available from the British Library.

10 9 8 7 6 5 4 3 2 1

Printed and bound by CPI Group (UK) Ltd, Croydon, CR0 4YY

To my beloved Corina
belonged for all eternities

who makes Eshq
real
to me

Contents

PATH OF LOVE

LOVER AND BELOVED

BELOVED COMMUNITY

Introduction: Islam's Path of Radical Love

The great mystic poet Farid al-Din 'Attar tells a moving story about a saint who had a vision of God in his dreams. In this vision, the whole of humanity, all who have ever been and shall ever be, are gathered before God. God presents them with a series of rewards that they can choose from. In the first offer, God asks them, "Who here wishes to have the totality of worldly desires?" Nine out of ten of those gathered choose these worldly pleasures. God says to them, "It is granted onto you," and they depart.

Of those who remain, God asks: "Who here wishes to be spared hellfire?" Again, nine out of ten raise their hands. God again says: "It is granted onto you," and they depart. Next, God asks the remaining minority who wishes to have a taste of heaven. Nine out of those who remain raise their hand, and God says to them: "It is granted onto you," and they depart.

At long last, there is but a handful of devoted lovers of God, not enchanted by worldly desires, unafraid of the torment of hellfire, and not seduced by the promise of paradise. This time the voice of God comes at them, thundering: "I offered you redemption from hellfire, you chose it not. I offered you my loftiest paradise, you chose it not. What, then, are you here for?"

They lowered their heads in humility and said:
"You. You yourself know Who we desire."

The mystics who seek God as a Beloved before all else, above heaven and hell, above salvation, spoke to God in intimate whispers and prayers overflowing with radical love called *Monajat.* This collection before you contains the love whispers of these select few who desire God above all else, and have found a way to God here and now through a love that emanates from God and is unleashed upon creation. All of us are told that we will meet God face to face in the Hereafter. These mystics are boldly impatient. They want to see the face of God Here and Now. The collection before you charts the poems and teachings of a path of radical love, *Eshq,* journeyed by Muslim sages, poets, dreamers, and lovers. It is this fierce love, a love divine mingling with humanity, that has been a means of spiritual ascension for these seekers who yearn to behold God here and now.

Here is a light-filled spark arising from the very heart of Muslim imagination, a poetic voice that looks to God through a bold love that is at once transformative and redemptive, human and divine. This mystical path, one called *Mazhab-e eshq* (Arabic: *madhhab al-'ishq*), is often translated as the "Path of Love," but that seems timid and insufficient. The word *love,* that most divine of qualities, has become flat, ubiquitous, and, ironically, cheap. No, the *Eshq* (in Persian: *'Eshq,* simplified here as *Eshq;* Arabic: *'Ishq*) that the Muslim mystics speak of is something more fiery, fierce, and alchemical. It is a love that by their own reckoning constantly spills over again and again, overflowing whatever cup seeks to contain it. It is for that reason that here I have rendered it as the path of radical love. The path of *Eshq* is the path of love that spills over again and again, and in a nod to the great jazz genius John Coltrane, we can call it the Path of Love Supreme. Like many jazz musicians, Coltrane had a deep fascination with Islam. Indeed many, myself included, have heard his masterpiece *A Love Supreme* as being also a chant of "Allah Supreme."

These love mystics have talked about the path (*Mazhab/ madhhab*) of radical love as being nothing less than God's own path, *mazhab-e khoda*. Hallaj (d. 922) and 'Ayn al-Qozat (d. 1131), both masters of this path of radical love, make this point explicitly. This path of radical love is the path that leads to God, as well as the path that God walks. Schools of Islamic law are named after the great scholars who consolidated their methodology; thus the Shafi'i madhhab is named after Imam al-Shafi'i, the Hanafi madhhab after Imam Abu Hanifa, the Ja'fari madhhab after Imam Ja'far Sadiq, and so on. But the path of radical love, the *Mazhab-e Eshq,* is not named after a mystic or a scholar, but is simply called God's own path. Here radical love and God are used interchangeably to denote love as the very essence of the divine.

The more precious something is, the more likely it is to be cheapened and abased. We have reduced love, this cosmic divine force, to a small sliver of its full potency. Nowadays when we speak about love, we almost exclusively refer to romantic love. But for the mystics, love is light. Love comes unabashedly, radiantly, in a thousand different shades and colors that still blend into One. There is love of the friend, the neighbor, the child, of the parent, the lover, the stranger, of God and the prophets, of saints and sinners, love of the self, love of the enemy, of nature, of realms seen and unseen. And more. For these mystics, love is fire. It is a purifying fire that burns away selfishness, greed, anger, ego, and leaves behind nothing but God.

For these love mystics, in order to know our own selves, we have to know God. To know God, we have to learn the mysteries of our own selves. And love is the key to unlocking these mysteries. The very mystery of existence is explained through divine love in a first-person saying attributed to the Prophet Muhammad. This genre that is referred to as Sacred Hadith, *Hadith Qudsi,* stands at the very heart of the mystical path, and has God revealed as a Hidden Treasure:

> *I was a Hidden treasure*
> *and I loved to be intimately known*
> *So I created the heavens and the earth*
> *that you may know Me*
> *Intimately.*

Here love is spoken of not as an emotion, not as a feeling or sentiment (though it fills up each of them and overflows). Rather, love is seen as nothing short of the very unleashing of God onto this realm of being. It is through love that God brings the cosmos into being, it is through love that we are sustained, and it is by merging with the cosmic current of love that we are led back Home.

In this saying God speaks in that intimate voice, the "I"

voice—not the transcendent "He," not the royal "We," but the deeply personal "I":

I was a Hidden treasure

and the phrase above translated as "I loved to be intimately known" is read as expressing a host of divine desires:

I loved,
I yearned,
I desired to be known intimately.

The root of the word for *love* here, God's yearning and desire to be known, *ahbabtu,* is said by some mystics to come from the word for bubbles, *hubab.* It is as if the love desire bubbled up inside God's own heart, turning and churning until even God could not restrain that desire anymore. This love rises up inside of God until it bursts forth as creation, a mighty big bang of love in the form of a desire to be known. There are many words in Arabic for knowledge, and the one used in this hadith, *u'rifa,* is to know intimately. God doesn't want to be known discursively, merely rationally, in the cool and distant intellect. God wants to be tasted and known in our bones. God is whispering to humanity: "I yearn to be tasted." The knowledge spoken of here is something more intimate, more immediate, more primal. It is a knowledge that mingles in our heart of hearts, uniting and uplifting all that makes us human.

In the first few centuries of Islam, the mystics attempted to divide love into two realms. They spoke of a *Eshq-e Haqiqi,* "real love," which was saved for God alone, and *Eshq-e Majazi,* "metaphorical love," which was the love that we as humans share with one another. According to these early mystics, human love was, in comparison with love for God, but a metaphor. It was as if we had to master the alphabet of human love before we would compose the great sonnet of divine love. That all changed with the eruption of the passionate path of radical love mystics, sages, poets, and seekers. These were the luminous souls who knew that there is, ultimately, One Love.

The mingling of this one love is what is reflected in the title of this collection: *Radical Love.* This radical love is reflected in a beautiful poem in which Rumi talks about this overflowing, spilling-over love as one that mingles between God and humanity, humanity and humanity, this world and that world, here and there, now and forever:

Look:
love mingles with Lovers

See:
spirit mingling with body

How long will you see life
as "this"
and "that"?

"Good"
and "bad"?

Look at how this
and that
are mingled

A love mingled and mingling. These mystics—referred to as
Sufis—saw themselves as reaching for the same mingled and
mingling radical love and luminous mercy that pours out
through the Qur'an. After all, does not every chapter of the
Qur'an (except for one) start with a reminder of how God's
mercy, compassion, and tenderness enfold the universe the way
that a mother contains an unborn child? While their path of a

radical love is certainly one that is universally resonant, it also has an unmistakable fragrance of the ascension of Muhammad. All Muslims aspire to emulate Muhammad's actions. These mystics yearned for more. As Muhammad rose to see God face to face, they too seek to ascend to see God face to face. All humanity will encounter God in the hereafter. These mystics want to see the Face of God here and now.

The path of radical love got its most clear articulation in a short meditative prose text called *Sawanih,* which reads like the love child of Platonic dialogues and Shakespearean sonnets in a Persian garden. The author is Ahmad Ghazali, the younger and much bolder brother of the famed Abu Hamid Muhammad Ghazali, often referred to as the most important Muslim theologian ever. The older brother is often considered on a par with Augustine and Aquinas, but it is the younger brother Ahmad who is the passionate and ecstatic love mystic who stands at a pinnacle of Islam's path of radical love. When the older Ghazali had his well-documented spiritual crisis and left for a few years of prayer and meditation in Jerusalem, the younger Ahmad took over the most distinguished professorship in the prestigious Nezamiyya madrasa, at the time perhaps the most esteemed institution of higher learning in the world. Ahmad was a superb preacher, mystic, and writer, patronized by the king and caliph alike. In our own age of vicious polemics against Islam and defensive apologetics it might seem hard to believe this, but at a zenith of Islamic civilization's political power it was a fiery passionate mystic whose sensual poetry was preached from the pulpit and university in Baghdad.

Ahmad Ghazali composed a short book called the *Sawanih* (Persian: *Savaneh*), which is a masterpiece of the path of radical love. Ahmad begins this book offering praise to God and the Prophet, and then immediately moves to discussing the mysteries of radical love, *Eshq.* He states that the reality of love cannot be captured in words. Undaunted, he conceives of his task through a beautiful and erotic metaphor. For him, writing about love is akin to creating a private wedding chamber in which the "men of words" can have union—with all of the sensual and spiritual connotations of the word—with the "virgin ideas" of radical love. For Ghazali, the inner reality of this supreme and overflowing love has remained untouched until then, but there would be union. In order for Ghazali to create this union, he has one condition for the reader. Ghazali will talk about the inner secrets of supreme love, provided that we not bifurcate love into a duality of human love and divine love. For Ghazali and the mystics of the path of love supreme, there would be One Love.

Later in the slim volume, Ghazali is even more specific about the connection between human love and divine love: He goes back to his favorite Qur'anic verse (with which he opens the very first chapter of *Sawanih*):

> *God loves them;*
> *They love God.*

QUR'AN 5:54

In Arabic, the word used here for love, *hubb,* looks like this:

There is a dot under the letter B in Arabic and Persian. Ahmad Ghazali goes back to the Qur'anic verse of "God loves them; they love God," and posits that the dot under the B in "God loves them" is planted in the "them" of humanity. It is the seed of love in this fertile heart's soil that leads to the flower of love in humanity. He concludes: this love is of the same color, *ham-rang,* the same essence, as that divine love. The seed has the same nature as the fruit, the fruit the same nature as the seed.

In a metaphor that changes how we think about love and spirit, Ghazali talks about the Spirit crossing over from the realm of nonexistence toward the realm of existence. When it gets to the very threshold of existence, love is already there awaiting the Spirit. In other words, love is preexisting, pre-eternal. This is consistent with the teachings of many mystics who see love not as merely another divine quality, but the divine quality par excellence, even perhaps equal to the being of God.

This love, a love that mingles between humanity and divinity, is not an emotion but a doing, a being, a becoming. It is a fire that cooks and burns, as Rumi is reported to have said:

> The whole of my life
> summed up in three phrases:
>
> I was raw
>
> then
> I was burnt
>
> Now,
> I am on fire

Perhaps a different way of putting it is to see love as alchemy. Our modern word *chemistry* comes from the Arabic for alchemy, which is not a pseudoscience or primitive science but rather a recognition that all of the cosmos shares in the same ultimate substance. Alchemists knew that each of us have something in us that is base like lead; yet everything in us that is cheap and base can be illuminated and become "gold"-like. Alchemy was ultimately the art of illumination and transformation. As Rumi says, it is through this radical love that the bitter becomes sweet, the thorn turns into a rose, the pain contains healing, and the dead come to life.

Ultimately, this radical love is channeled through humanity. It has to be lived and embodied, shared and refined not in the heavens but right here and now, in the messiness of earthly life. The path to God goes through that most difficult of beings, the human being. God is easy. We as human beings are hard.

Rumi's biography tells the story beautifully. He had a devotee who was born as a Christian named Seryanus, and took the name Aladdin ('Ala al-Din) as a Muslim. Seryanus, pulled by the magnetic flame of love that burns through Rumi, had converted to Islam and attempted to learn Rumi's language, Persian. Yet like so many of us who have attempted to express our deepest yearning and highest aspiration in a second and third language, he kept using the wrong words in Persian. Like Victorian English that distinguished between calling a human being "lord" and calling God "Lord," Persian had words that could refer to the lord of a village or Lord of the cosmos. The poor simpleton Seryanus kept referring to Rumi as "Lord." Some fanatical people in town dragged him before a judge, putting him through an inquisition, wondering why he was calling Rumi—a mere mortal—by the exalted title "Lord." Seryanus, flustered, retorted: "I always do this. I am so sorry, I didn't mean to call him Lord." The judge, momentarily satisfied, held off and said: "What did you mean to call him?" Seryanus confidently answered: *khodaa-saaz,* "God-maker"!

Justified in the accusers' belief that Seryanus was in fact a heretic, the judge was willing to sign off on having the new convert put to death. Seryanus said again:

> I always do this. I am so sorry.
> I call him God-maker, because he makes God . . .
>> He makes God real to me.
> Before I met him, God was a name that I called upon by blindly following others.

Now

I know that God is real.

The history of Islam, like the histories of all religious traditions, is filled with these human beings who make God real, make love real, and let love shine. This collection of the teachings of the path of supreme love, radical love, one love, consists of four units. The first unit, "God of Love," looks at the ultimate teachings that locate the source of radical love not just in God, but as God. The second, "Path of Radical Love," looks at the meditations on this overflowing fiery supreme and radical love. The third, "Lover and Beloved," looks at the dance of love, this being and becoming. The last, "Beloved Community," looks at the path of love not merely as one toward God, but also one of forming a beautiful community, a loving community, a beloved community here and now.

For the mystics of the path of love, this locating of God in the very midst of humanity is reflected in how they read the Qur'an. One example will suffice here. The Arabic language of the Qur'an did not use commas and periods. There are many places in the Qur'an where pausing after one word instead of another can radically change the meaning of the whole verse.

One of the clear examples is in the verse that is often employed upon hearing of a death. The verse addresses the "souls at peace," who are pleased with God as God is pleased with them. The most obvious way of reading the verse is:

Enter inside,
O My servants,
and you have entered My garden.

But many mystics, including Rumi, read the same verse differently. In reading it, as it were, without a comma, they arrive at a radically different, and more powerful, reading:

Enter inside My servants,
and you have entered My garden.

In this reading, God's supreme reward, the garden of paradise, is found when we enter inside the heart of one of God's beloveds, those who are pleased with God and with whom God is pleased. In this mystical reading, the garden is not a physical destination but a spiritual state that we discover here and now.

O soul at peace
return to your Lord

You pleased with God
God pleased with you

Enter inside My servants,
you have entered My garden.

QUR'AN 89:27–30

This too is part of the path of love, where God's supreme pleasure, the highest paradise, is attainable here and now, inside the hearts of God's loving devotees.

Love is not merely an emotion, but the very unleashing of God on Earth. It is one that shapes our individual soaring to God as much as it shapes what it means to live in harmony with one another in a beloved community. To live in a beloved community takes harmony, and a commitment to sharing finite resources in a way that guarantees the dignity of all, meeting the needs of everyone. That harmony we call justice. Many traditions link together the dimensions of love and social justice. In Islam the realm of spirituality, *Ihsan,* rendered in the verse below as "love," literally means to bring into reality what is good and beautiful. *Ihsan,* the dimension of love, harmony, and beauty, is a commitment to realize and actualize love here and now. To be spiritually awake, we have to make goodness and beauty real.

In a popular Prophetic tradition, *Ihsan* stands for the aspect of the path to God that is higher than "whole-hearted surrender to God" (*Islam*) and "faith" (*Iman*). In the Qur'anic verse below, the divine command links together this dimension of love, mercy, and beauty (*Ihsan*) with that of social justice, in a way that is reminiscent of the American civil rights tradition: when love enters the public square, we call it justice.

> *This is God's command:*
> *love and justice.*

QUR'AN 16:90

In this Qur'anic verse, God commands humanity to both *Ihsan* (rendered here as "love") and justice. Love and justice are seen as being intrinsically connected. This radical love is one that moves inward and shows up as tenderness, and pours outward and shines as justice. To be a mystic of the path of radical love necessitates tenderness in our intimate dealings, and a fierce commitment to social justice in the community we live in, both local and global.

On Translation

Translations of Sufi material have tended to suffer from two tendencies. One genre has been that of literal, word-for-word translations from Victorian scholars such as R. A. Nicholson and A. J. Arberry, who boasted that their works have been "as literal as possible, with a minimal concession to readability." On the other hand, we have the "versions" of contemporary translators who are working not from the original Persian/Arabic but rather from the literal Victorian translations. In many cases, they have sought to minimize the Islamic context and cast these poems into a generic, universal model of spirituality. In a few cases, such as almost all the material attributed to Rumi and Hafez online, there is no earthly historical connection between these materials and anything the mystic poets of history ever uttered. This is particularly the case for the material attributed to Hafez.

In all the material in this collection, I have referred back to the original sources, and sought to provide a new English translation that is evocative, fresh, accurate, and poetic. It has to read as poetry in the new host language, and convey something of the fire and spirit of the original, while preserving the symbols and references. In some cases I have decided that a whole *ghazal* (a sonnet) may not work in English, but a shorter selection from the poem does. The section for sources at the end of this volume will enable those with access to the original languages to trace them back to the primary sources.

This Collection

The mystics of Islam see themselves as being rooted unambiguously in the word of God (the Qur'an) and the very being of the Prophet. If I may be permitted a neologism, their poems and stories are "Qur'an-ful," filled with both direct and indirect references to scripture. Mawlana Jalal al-Din Balkhi (known in the West as Rumi), the luminous sage of radical love whose poetry graces this collection more than any other writer's, speaks of his own work the *Masnavi* as being one that repeatedly and emphatically unveils the beauty of the Qur'an. This unveiling is both sensual and intellectual. The metaphor is quite literally one of unveiling a bride at the night of union before achieving oneness. It is a *dis-covering,* an uncovering, of the literal meaning of scripture to yield the infinite layers of inner meaning filled with pleasure, wonder, and beauties. The very act of reading scripture, and reading one's own heart, becomes a pursuit of pleasure and discovery. Without these mystical guides the bride of scripture remains veiled, her beauty unseen, unknown, and untasted.

The mystics also have a direct relationship with the Prophet Muhammad. All Muslims claim to follow the Prophet's example, *Sunna*. The mystics also claim a connection with the very being of the Prophet, the light of the Prophet. Even in his own lifetime, Rumi was referred to as the "offspring of the Soul of Muhammad." There have been Sunni Sufis and Shi'i Sufis, and collectively they have sought to bring unity to humanity by transcending sectarianism. Whereas all Muslims, including mystically inclined Muslims, emulate the actions of the Prophet, it is the mystics who want the experience of the Prophet in seeing God face to face. All of us will have to encounter God in the hereafter; the mystics are merely more impatient. The purpose of Muhammad's ascension, *Mi'raj,* was to behold the face of God. These radical love mystics, the inheritors of the light of Muhammad, also want to encounter God here and now.

Some Qur'anic verses posit Muhammad as a being of cosmic significance. Key among them is the following verse, which states that Muhammad was sent as a mercy not only to this universe but to all the universes, all the cosmos, all the realms seen and unseen:

> *We sent you*
> *Muhammad*
> *as a mercy*
> *To all the universes*

QUR'AN 21:107

The texts that identify these cosmic qualities of Muhammad are recorded not only in the customary collections that all Muslims (Sunni and Shi'a) honor, but particularly through a special subset of prophetic statements known as *Hadith Qudsi* or Sacred Hadith. These are purported to be private communications between Muhammad and God that convey the inner mysteries of the path of radical love. In one such *Hadith Qudsi,* God reveals to Muhammad how Divine love for Muhammad is the very secret of creation. It is not merely that God is the "Hidden Treasure" that yearns, loves, and desires to be known. Muhammad himself is named as the cause of all creation in the famed *lawlak* (If not for you . . .):

If not for you, O Muhammad,
I would not have created the Heavens.

HADITH QUDSI

Every tradition is a flowing stream. No tradition is static. Truth is continuously and perpetually revealed, and there have been thousands of women and men over the centuries whose yearning for God bears the fragrance of the path of Muhammad. This collection also includes many of these intimate friends of God, the *awliya'.* Here are some of their most prominent members who stand out in this collection.

The Mystics

Mawlana Jalal al-Din Balkhi (d. 1273), known as Rumi in the West. He is the masterful poet and saint who has left an immense spiritual impact on Persia, South Asia, Central Asia, and Turkey. He was born in the region where present-day Afghanistan and Central Asia meet, journeyed through Persia, and lived the rest of his days in Konya (present-day Turkey). His masterpiece, the *Masnavi,* has had such an unrivaled impact on Muslims' imagination that it came to be called the "Qur'an in Persian." His lyrical collection of love poems, dedicated to his theophanic spiritual mentor, Shams-e Tabrizi, is called the *Divan-e Kabir* or *Divan-e Shams,* and has been a favorite of Sufi musicians for centuries. The Sufi community that traces itself to him—known as the *Mevlevis,* or Whirling Dervishes—is particularly well known in the West, due to its iconic whirling, meditative dance. With one foot remaining stationary and one in motion, the dervish connects together the Earth and Heaven, reminding the audience of the need to balance motion and stillness.

Abu 'Abd al-Rahman Muhammad ibn al-Husayn al-Sulami. Al-Sulami, who died in 1021, was a key figure in identifying the *adab* (compassionate, selfless behavior) that has been seen as much more than merely a component of the Path: it has been equated with the whole of the Sufi path. His *Tabaqat al-Sufiyya* is considered one of the most important collections of stories about the lives of early Muslim mystics. He compiled a lovely little book, *Kitab al-Futuwwa* (translated as *The Way of Sufi Chivalry*) which identifies the etiquette of being in a Sufi community. Here chivalry has nothing to do with wearing armor or being a knight, but rather with the ideals of compassion, generosity, selflessness, and kindness. Another work by al-Sulami, *Dhikr al-muta'abbidat al-sufiyyat,* has been translated by Rkia E.

Cornell as *Early Sufi Women.* This work provides us with evidence that contrary to earlier assumptions, there was much more to the participation of women in the Sufi path than the brief anecdotes of the noted female saint Rabi'a.

Abu 'l-Hasan Kharaqani (d. 1033), a bold mystic from the town of Kharaqan (present-day Iran), is one of the gentlest lovers on the path of radical love. It was Kharaqani who wrote: "Whoever falls in love passionately, a radical love that spills over, finds God." And the tale from Kharaqani in this collection, "A Deal with God," gives an indication of his loving, tender, friendly relationship with God. Kharaqani is the very embodiment of the definition of the path of love as being "at ease with God."

Abu Sa'id-e Abi 'l-Khayr (d. 1037) is yet another of the towering mystics from the region of Khorasan. He spent much of his life around the region of Nishapur (in Khorasan, present-day Iran), and is often credited with establishing much of the communal life of mystics in the form of the Sufi lodge, *khanaqah.* The fact that the term for the Sufi communal gathering is said to share a root with the word *khana,* meaning "home," gives a sense of the "homey" feeling a Sufi community should have. Abu Sa'id famously said that a real saint is not one who flies in the air or walks on water, but simply one who continues to be fully present with God in every breath even in the midst of work and family.

Ahmad Ghazali (d. 1126) spent his life moving from the region of Khorasan to Baghdad and Qazvin, covering modern-day Iran and 'Iraq. The younger brother of the more famed Imam Abu Hamid Muhammad Ghazali (d. 1111), Ahmad, is the author of the first book in Persian on radical love, called *Sawanih* (*Savaneh*). It is in the *Sawanih,* as we have seen, that Ahmad makes a bold claim: there is but One Love. Ghazali promises to write a book of love provided there is no distinction made between divine love and human love. Whereas previous Sufis talked about a distinction between real love (love of God) and metaphorical love (love among humanity), Ahmad Ghazali posits One Love, a divine love that preceded creation, overflows to bring us here, sustains us here, and will deliver us back home.

'Ayn al-Qudat Hamadhani, or 'Ayn al-Qozat Hamadani (d. 1131), was a student and disciple of Ahmad Ghazali. The brilliant and fiery 'Ayn al-Qozat fleshes out the path of radical love by making explicit much of what had been implicit before. Whereas Ahmad Ghazali wrote in pithy poetic maxims, 'Ayn al-Qozat provided the subtle connections to verses of the Qur'an and the teachings of the Prophet, earlier Sufi poetry, and his own genius interpretation. While 'Ayn al-Qozat lived in western Iran, his writings on the path of radical love were studied by Rumi and his circle in Turkey, in India, and elsewhere. In particular, 'Ayn al-Qozat's masterpiece, the *Tamhidat,* is one of the supreme gems of the path of radical love. 'Ayn al-Qozat, who was called the Sultan of Radical Love by later Sufis, was martyred at the age of thirty-three for his bold political critique of unjust rulers. Despite the brevity of his life, he stands out as one of the most original giants of love mysticism in Islam.

Mosleh al-Din Sa'di (d. 1291 or 1292) was from Shiraz, in Iran. The *Rose Garden* (*Golestan*) of Sa'di epitomized what it has meant to be a refined soul in the eastern part of the Muslim majority world for the better part of the last millennium. The text's anecdotes and proverbs perfume the soul of Persian-speaking Muslims, and have become the very model of elegant prose impregnated by beautiful poetry. While Sa'di is usually relegated to the realm of "humanism" or "ethics," he also has much to say about mystics and the path of love. As is worthy of a sophisticated thinker, he recognizes that there are saints and charlatans among those claiming to be Sufis. After all, is it not the case that the more precious a subject, the more likely there are to be forgeries and imitations? There are fake gold coins, but no fake pennies. It is also Saʿdi who most directly connects the message of kindness and tenderness to a broad humanism. Every Persian speaker knows by heart his maxim "Humanity is like members of one body, created out of the same essence." Far fewer know that Saʿdi was merely translating and paraphrasing the humanistic wisdom of the Prophet Muhammad, who expressed the same truth in a hadith. Saʿdi is also the master of sublime love sonnets, several of which are translated here.

Fakhr al-Din ʿIraqi was another of the giants of the path of radical love. He hailed from Hamadan in western Iran, and died in 1289. More or less a contemporary of Rumi, he marked the trend that consisted of blending together the love mysticism of the path of radical love with the lofty metaphysics of the Andalusian mystic Ibn ʿArabi. It was ʿIraqi's *Lamaʿat* (translated as *Divine Flashes*) which became a much beloved and commented upon masterpiece everywhere in the Persian world.

His sensual writings spoke of a beloved in the most tender

terms: "You are my life and soul. Without you, I don't breathe well." He theorized how the Divine Beloved would be manifested in the form of human lovers and beloveds. Significantly for gender purposes, 'Iraqi understood that God is revealed in both male and female forms, both "Adam" and "Eve." 'Iraqi boldly proclaims God as being none other than radical love (*Eshq*), and even expressed a distinctly mystical notion of the "Trinity," in which love, lover, and beloved are all seen as One, as none other than God.

By some accounts, the poetry collection of Khwaja Shams al-Din Muhammad Hafez of Shiraz (d. 1390) known as the *Divan-e Hafez* is among the most widely circulated texts in the history of Islam. Hafez is the great master of ambiguity, sensuality, and spiritual intoxication. His honorific "Hafez" indicates one who has committed the whole of the Qur'an to heart, yet another reminder of the intimate relationship between love mystics and scripture. No other poet is as intent on locating passionate ecstatic love here and now, in this very realm, as much as in the eternities to come. Hafez loathes spiritual hypocrisy, and mocks those who perform acts of piety to impress the gullible. But he is a seeker after God's

own heart, one who sees the divine in the form of his earthly
beloveds:

> A roselike beauty
> in my embrace
>
> Wine
> at hand
>
> Beloved,
> pleased
>
> Next to me
> the sultan of the whole world
> would be a servant

Hafez recognizes that love is the divine keepsake. It is simulta-
neously the unleashing of God onto this realm, and a reminder
of that divine origin:

> I've heard
> nothing lovelier
> than the melody of love
>
> a keepsake
> lingering

> in this whirling
> azure dome

Farid al-Din 'Attar (d. 1221) too arises from that rich region of Khorasan, present-day Iran, home to so many giants in the realm of the spirit. Perhaps no other early figure has done as much to weave together poetry and Sufism in the path of radical love. His *Manteq al-tayr,* ("Conference of the Birds"), is a mystical allegory of the journey of a group of birds to behold God. Like the journey of the birds—which in so many traditions symbolize spirits—the journey of mystics is not an individual one but a collective one. When the birds arrive at the zenith of their journey they find the Ultimate Beloved to be but a reflection of their own selves. Indeed, as the Prophet said, to know God we have to know ourselves.

Yet they act surprised, unsure, and perhaps even unworthy. They complain that there is no clear path before them. And as 'Attar says, it is when we take the first step on the path of love that the path appears under our feet. Perhaps this is how it has to be: we must begin.

As the birds of the spirit in 'Attar's tale soared together, I invite you to join us on this journey of love. May you find in these poems, in these luminous and fierce teachings of radical love from the heart of the Islamic tradition a mirror—one to reflect to you the beauty of your own soul.

Look!
This is love
—to soar toward the heavens

GOD OF LOVE

For the mystics of the path of radical love, love (*Eshq*) is not a sentiment or an emotion. It is the very overflowing of God onto this realm. It is this radical love that erupts out of God, bringing us into being. It is this love that sustains us, and it will be this cosmic current that will carry us back home.

God may have a hundred names, but the qualities of love, mercy, kindness, and tenderness are the very essence of God's own being.

God's qualities of love and mercy flow through fully realized human beings. The light of God shines in prophets and saintly beings, particularly Muhammad, who has been sent as a mercy to all the different universes.

Whichever Way You Turn

To God belong
all that is in the East
and in the West

God's is the place of sun rising
and the place of sun setting

So whichever way you turn
there is His face
there's His core being

He wraps around you
He knows. . . .

QUR'AN

One Love

Soon God will bring forth a people
He will love them
they will love Him

QUR'AN

Not This, Not That
Both This and That

I will write you a book on Radical Love
provided you do not bifurcate it
into Divine Love
and Human Love

AHMAD GHAZALI

The Opening

We begin in the Name of God
Everlasting Mercy, Infinite Compassion

Praise be to God
Loving Lord of all the worlds

Everlasting Mercy
Infinite Compassion

Eternal Strength of every living being,
Whose Majestic Power embraces us on the day of the great
    return

Only You do we adore, and to You alone do we cry for help

Guide us, O God, on the path of Perfect Harmony,
the path of those whom You have blessed with the gifts of
    Peace, Joy,
Serenity and Delight

the path of those who are not brought down by grief-stricken
    rage,

the path of those who are not lost along the way

Amin!
So be it.

QUR'AN

Love and Justice

This is God's command:
love & justice

QUR'AN

A God Closer Than . . .

I created humanity
I know what whispers into your soul . . .
and I am closer to you
than the beating of your heart

QUR'AN

God Intervenes

God intervenes between
a man
and his ever-changing heart

QUR'AN

Signs of God

We shall show them our Signs
on the horizons
and inside their own souls
until it becomes clear to them
that He
is God;

God
is Truth

QUR'AN

Enter Inside My Servants

O soul at peace
return to your Lord

You pleased with God
God pleased with you

Enter inside My servants,
you have entered My Garden

QUR'AN

Remembrance of God

The remembrance of God
brings serenity
to hearts

QUR'AN

Never Give Up Hope

O My servants
who have sinned
            against your own souls
Never give up hope
            Of God's mercy
He forgives sins
            altogether
He is All-Forgiving,
            Ever-Merciful

QUR'AN

Face of God

Everything on the Earth
is perpetually vanishing

But the face of your cherishing Lord
remains

Full of splendor
and grace

QUR'AN

Wherever

God is with you
wherever you are

QUR'AN

Where Is God?

Muhammad was once asked:
"Where is God?"

He answered:
"In the hearts of His servants"

HADITH

Muhammad as Mercy

We sent you
Muhammad
as a mercy
to all the universes

QUR'AN

Perfect Our Light

Our Lord!
Perfect our Light for us
and grant us forgiveness . . .

QUR'AN

God's Mercy

God has proscribed upon Himself:

"Indeed My mercy comes before,
goes after,
and takes over My wrath"

HADITH QUDSI

Hidden Treasure

I was a Hidden Treasure
and I yearned,
I *loved*
to be known
      intimately

So I created the heavens and the Earth
so that they may know Me
      intimately

HADITH QUDSI

God, Love, and Beauty

God is beautiful
and loves beauty

HADITH

Show Mercy

All-Merciful God
shows mercy
to those who are merciful

Show mercy to those on Earth
and the Heavens will show you mercy

HADITH

For the Sake of Muhammad

If not for you,
Muhammad,
I would not have created
the Heavens

HADITH QUDSI

A Heart to Contain God

My Heaven cannot contain Me
neither can My Earth

But the heart
of My faithful devotee
suffices Me

HADITH QUDSI

Uninterrupted Lightning

When the lights of Divine self-revelation
      manifest to the heart
it is clear
      and uninterrupted
Like
lightning
      in the middle of a starless night
The night
      turns into day

ʿAMR IBN ʿUTHMAN AL-MAKKI

A Moment

I have this eternal moment
             this very Now
with God
a moment
             so intimate
that there is no room for
any angel brought near
or any prophet sent down

HADITH

Know Thyself

To know God
intimately

intimately
know yourself

"He who knows his own soul
knows his Lord"

HADITH QUDSI

God Sees Your Hearts

God does not look at your external form
and not your actions

God casts loving glances
toward your hearts

HADITH

Lord of the Ka'ba

Rabi'a was heading for pilgrimage toward Mecca.

In the middle of the desert,
she saw that the house of God,
the Ka'ba itself,
had come to welcome her.

She said:

"I need the Lord of the House.
      What am I to do with the Ka'ba?"

FARID AL-DIN 'ATTAR

Removing Dirt from the Path

Master 'Abd al-Karim, who used to serve Abu Sa'id, said that when he was a child, his father brought him to Abu Sa'id. Abu Sa'id subtly looked over at a piece of trash that was in the Sufi lodge, and pointed to it. 'Abd al-Karim went over and picked it up.

The Shaykh said: "Bring it over."
He said: "What do you call this in your language?"
I said: "Trash."

The Shaykh said: "Know that this world and the hereafter are the trash on the path to the Beloved. Until you remove the trash from the path, you cannot arrive at the goal."

This is why the Leader of the World (Prophet Muhammad), peace and blessings be upon him, said: "The lowest level of faith is to remove the dirt from the path."

Then he said:
"Whatever is not of God, is no-thing.
Whoever is not of God, is no-one."

Wherever you are with your notion of "you,"
    that's hell.
Wherever you discard your notion of "you,"
    that's heaven.

ABU SAʿID-E ABI ʾL-KHAYR

Divine Qualities

Adorn yourself
With Divine Qualities

HADITH QUDSI

Beloved So Close to Me

The Beloved is closer to me
Than my own self

The problem is this:
I am far from Him

What am I to do?
Whom can I tell about this?

The Beloved is so close to me
and I
am far

      far away

SA'DI

Be at Ease

The Path is

To be at ease
with God

SAHL AL-TOSTARI

The Heart of Your Friend

O God,
In this world I sinned,
which saddened your friend,
            Muhammad,
               and delighted your enemy,
             Satan

If you punish me in the next world
it would yet again sadden your friend
               Muhammad
and again delight your enemy
               Satan

Do not sadden the heart of your friend
twice

Forgive

KHWAJA ʿABDULLAH ANSARI

Something Else

I've searched from horizon to horizon
Seeking the love of beautiful souls
Seen lots of good and beautiful ones
But you
Muhammad
You
are something else

SABRI BROTHERS

Saying "I"

Only God
has the right
to say "I"

ABU BAKR KHARRAZ

Forgiveness

A secret whisper came to me
from the Tavern's corner

"Drink!
He forgives."

God's grace is bigger
than my sin

HAFEZ

You Are Greater

My sin is great,
but You are greater than my sin

ABU ʿABD AL-RAHMAN MUHAMMAD
IBN AL-HUSAYN AL-SULAMI

God in Search of Humanity

He who seeks Me
finds Me

He who seeks other than Me
will never find me

Pious souls yearn to behold Me
I yearn more to behold them

HADITH QUDSI

A Single Breath

To take a single breath
in the presence of God
is greater than all the treasures on Earth
or in Heaven

'ATTAR

It's All Him!

The throne is on the water
The whole world is up in the air
Forget water and air:
It's all God!

The throne and the world
are nothing other than talismans
to conjure Him

He alone is,
other than Him
there is nothing but names.

Look carefully!
This world,
that world
are all Him!

There is nothing other than Him.
And if there was,
even that
is also Him!

It's all one Essence
defined through His attributes

To be a man of God
you have to know your King
even if you see your King
in a hundred robes

'ATTAR

Muhammad, the Maternal Prophet

I am like that child
swirling around in water
anxious
I flail my arms around

Be generous!
right now
cast a compassionate glance
to us children of the path
who are drowning

Have mercy
on our anxious hearts
save us from this water
through your kindness and grace

Suckle us
from your breast of generosity

Don't keep from us
this feast of grace

'ATTAR

At Last

I searched and searched and searched
and I could not find Thee anywhere

I called Thee aloud, standing on the minaret
I rang the temple bell
       with the rising and setting of the sun

I bathed in Ganges in vain
I came back from Ka'ba disappointed

I looked for Thee in heaven
my Beloved, my Pearl

But at last I have found Thee
hidden in the shell of my heart.

HAZRAT INAYAT KHAN

Heart, Lord

Finding my Lord
I lost my heart

Finding my heart
I lost my Lord

ABU 'L-HUSAYN AL-NURI

No Way to Treat a Friend

Rabi'a said:

O my God!
If tomorrow
you send me to hell
I'll cry out:
"I loved you!
        Is this how you treat your friends?"

The voice of God responded:
"O Rabi'a!
        Don't think so poorly of Me!

I'll raise you among My friends
        so you and I can speak!"

RABI'A

Forgive Freely!

My God!
You created freely
gave me sustenance freely
so forgive freely!

You are God
not an accountant

ANSARI

God's Path

They asked Hallaj:
"Which path do you follow?"

He answered:
"God's path"

FAKHR AL-DIN ʿIRAQI

Love, Harmony, and Beauty

Praise be to Thee, Most Supreme God,
Omnipotent, Omnipresent, All-pervading,
the Only Being.

Take us in Thy Parental Arms,
raise us from the denseness of the earth,

Thy Beauty do we worship,
to Thee do we give willing surrender.

Most Merciful and Compassionate God,
the Idealized Lord of the whole humanity,

Thee only do we worship, and toward Thee Alone we aspire.
Open our hearts toward Thy Beauty

Illuminate our souls with Divine Light,
O Thou, the Perfection of Love, Harmony and Beauty,
All-powerful Creator, Sustainer,
Judge and Forgiver of our shortcomings,
Lord God of the East and of the West,

of the worlds above and below,
and of the seen and unseen beings:

Pour upon us Thy Love and Thy Light,
give sustenance to our bodies, hearts and souls,

use us for the purpose that Thy Wisdom chooseth,
and guide us on the path of Thine Own Goodness.

Draw us closer to Thee every moment of our life,
until in us be reflected Thy Grace, Thy Glory,
Thy Wisdom, Thy Joy and Thy Peace.
Amen.

HAZRAT INAYAT KHAN

Prayer of Rabi'a

O Lord,

If I worship you
for fear of hell
burn me in that hell

If I worship you
hoping for paradise,
make it forbidden for me

But if I worship you
only for your own sake
Do not withhold from me
your everlasting beauty

RABI'A

This and That

You are manifest
you are hidden
both

Not *this*
not *that*

Yet . . .

This,
and *that.*

How can you be manifest
when you're always hidden?

How can you be hidden
when you're eternally plain to see?

ʿIRAQI

Lord of the Path

A man said to Shaykh Yahya ibn Mu'adh al-Razi:

You know
so much about the spiritual path

yet are so ignorant
about the Lord of the Path

ABU SA'ID

No Heaven, No Hell

O my God
how good would it be
if there were no heaven
and no hell

So we'd see
who truly
worships you

ABU 'L-HASAN KHARAQANI

But I Know

'Attar tells the story of how Gabriel heard God's tender
response of "I am with you" coming from the highest realm of
Paradise. He wondered which servant of God would deserve
such a response. All that Gabriel knew was that it had to be one
of a high spiritual rank, one who had rid himself of his ego,
and had an awake heart. Gabriel looked all over the seven
heavens, in the sea, and in the oceans. Yet again he looked all
over the cosmos, and found no one to match that lofty rank. So
he asked God to guide him. God said to go to Byzantium, and
look in the monastery. Gabriel came there, and found one
person who was bowing down before an idol, weeping. He
returned to God, and said:

O you without need, unveil this mystery for me!
How can it be that this one is calling on an idol,
and you're answering through your grace?

God Almighty said: His heart is not filled with light.
He doesn't know.
Not knowing,
he's gone astray.

He went wrong,
being ignorant.

But I know.
Since I know,
I'll show him the way.

'Attar ends with a reassuring line for the sinful reader:

If you have nothing to bring to this exalted court
fear not.
He doesn't buy
every pious act of self-denial.

If you have nothing
He buys nothingness.

'ATTAR

Seeing Nothing Other than God

Humanity can reach such a rank
that we see
nothing other than God

Look at how lofty
is the rank of humanity!

SAʿDI

God's Not Lost

If you search for God
day and night

and can't find Him
Your seeking
is lacking

He's not lost

'ATTAR

My Only Shame

My only shame
is this

On the Day of Judgment
I won't have sinned
enough
to match
the enormity
of Your forgiveness

QA'ANI

Door Never Closed

A man
not knowing
said to God:

"O God
at long last
open a door for me."

Rabi'a was there:

"You fool!

The door's
never
been closed."

RABI'A

A Deal with God

One night Abu 'l-Hasan Kharaqani was praying to God.

He heard a voice from beyond:
"O Abu 'l-Hasan!
Do you want Me to tell people
everything I know about you,
       so that they stone you?"

Shaykh Kharaqani answered back to God:
"O my God!
Do you want me to tell them everything I know
about your loving mercy and forgiveness,
everything I see from your generosity?
If I do,
no one would ever bother with acts of worship,
no one would prostrate in prayer!"

The voice of God answered:

*"You say nothing;
I say nothing"*

KHARAQANI

Where Do You See God?

They asked Kharaqani:
"Where do you see God?"

He said:
"Wherever I don't see myself"

KHARAQANI

My Only Need

Rayhana "the Enraptured," an eighth-century female mystic, had this poem inscribed inside her collar:

> You are my intimate friend
> my aspiration
> my joy
>
> My heart
> refuses
> to love
> other than you
>
> O my dear
> my aspiration
> all I desire . . .
>
> My yearning for you
> grows and grows
> when can I see you?
>
> I desire not
> that Lofty Paradise

All I desire
is to see your face

RAYHANA "THE ENRAPTURED"

Seeing God

This is what it means
to see God

That you see nothing
other than Him

KHARAQANI

God's Lap

The mystics are
children
in God's lap

SHEBLI

Everywhere You Look

Everywhere you look
there is God

Look beneath:
God

Look above:
God

Look to the right:
God

Look to the left:
God

Look behind you:
God

Look in front of you:
God

KHARAQANI

Finding God

Whoever falls in love
passionately

a radical love
that spills over

finds God

KHARAQANI

PATH OF LOVE

Whereas many religious traditions speak of God as the Lord, the King, and the Master, the mystics call on God also as a friend (*doost*), a lover, and a beloved.

Whereas many speak of the human quest for God, those who walk on the path of love know that God is also seeking humanity.

Rather than merely a vertical relationship of submission, the path of love becomes a sensual and spiritual love affair of seeking and yearning, being and becoming, among God and humanity.

Say Nothing

I serve
that moonlike beauty
say nothing to me
unless it's about her

Speak nothing of sorrow
Say nothing other than these treasured words

Last night I became
love-crazed

Love saw me
and said:
I've come
don't shout
say nothing

I said:
Love,
I'm afraid of something else

Love said:
There *is* nothing else
Say nothing!

Let me whisper secrets
in your ear
Say nothing!

I said:
What a beauty!
Are you
an angel
or a human?

Love said:
Not an angel
not a human
Say nothing!

I said:
What is this?
Say it!

Love said:
Stay like this
Say nothing!

I said:
My heart . . . Have mercy!
Aren't you describing
God??

Love said:
Yes, my child,
But *hush!*

Say nothing

JALAL AL-DIN BALKHI (RUMI)

Muhammad on Perfume, Women, and Prayer

I was made to love
Three things from this world of yours:

Perfume,
women,
but that which delights my soul
is prayer

HADITH

Water Takes on the Color of the Cup

> She who knows her own self
> knows her Lord
>
> This is why Junayd said:
> Water takes on the color of the cup

'IRAQI

Many Paths to the Ka'ba

The paths
are many
The destination
is one

Do you not see?
There are many paths
to the Ka'ba

RUMI

Pain

How do you ever expect
for your heart to become polished
like a mirror
without putting up
with the pain
of polish?

RUMI

Looking for God in Hearts

The Prophet tells us
what God has said

"I cannot fit
above
or below

My Earth
My Heaven
My Throne
contain Me not

Know this for sure
my dear . . .
what wonder!

The heart
of My faithful servant
suffices Me

If you seek Me
look for me inside
these hearts"

HADITH QUDSI/RUMI

A Love Beyond Time

I swim inside
this love
on my inside

Love that was
before there was a time

Love that will be
after there will be a time

RUMI

Accept Whatever Comes from God

God is
like the soul

This world
like His body

Accept whatever comes
from the soul

RUMI

Everything Sings

We have loved
passionately

A love that spills over

Everything we are
sings

ABU SAʿID

An Awake Heart

My eyes
sleep

My heart's
awake

HADITH

Martyr of Love

Whoever loves passionately
and keeps that love chaste
and hides it
and dies in that love
has died the death of a martyr

HADITH

Mi'raj (Heavenly Ascension)

Radical Love
is an ascension

taking us to the roof
to rendezvous
with the Sultan of beauty

Read on a lover's face
the tale of
this rising

RUMI

I Want Not to Want

A long-suffering soul was asked:
"What does your heart want?"

He said:
"That my heart not desire anything"

SA'DI

Nothing Owns You

The Sufi path is this:

You own
nothing

Nothing
owns you

ABU NASR AL-SARRAJ

Joy Inside the Heart

What is the Sufi path?

"To find joy
inside the inner heart
when sadness
comes"

RUMI

Ocean of Sorrow

In the midst
of an ocean of sorrow

Love
is sorrowless

RUMI

A Blazing Lightning

The path is:
a blazing lightning bolt
that burns up
everything

SHEBLI

Leaping Heavenward

In every breath
comes love's calling
from every way

I am leaping heavenward
Who wants to watch?

From the Heavens
I come

The King's friend
I am

I wanna go back
to that place
that's my home

RUMI

A Secret

There is a secret
hidden
in the heart of God's people

That secret
even Gabriel
cannot find

Seek it

RUMI

Wordless Secrets

I hushed my mouth
closed door to speech

But tonight
it's me
with no words
speaking secrets

RUMI

Endless Beloved

The great mystic Zol Nun met a woman at the seashore.
He asked her: "What is the end of love?"

She answered:
"O simpleton, love has no end"

He asked: "Why?"

She answered:
"Because God
the Beloved
has no end"

ZOL NUN

Sound of One-Handed Clapping

No lover would seek union
If the beloved
were not seeking her . . .

When the lightning bolt of love for the friend
has shot into *this* heart
Know this:

There is also love
in *that* heart

When love for God doubles
in your heart
have no doubt!
God also
loves you

Have you ever heard
the sound of one-handed clapping?

A thirsty man moans:
"O precious water!"

Water also moans:
"Who wants to drink me?"

RUMI

Power of the Words of Love

The great Sumnun, known as "the lover," went to Hijaz.
The people of Fayd asked him:
"Say some words for us."

Sumnun went up on the pulpit,
but didn't find anyone who was really able to truly hear what
he had to say.

So he faced the chandelier of the mosque, and addressed them:
"I will speak with you about love."

The chandeliers
            shattered.

SUMNUN

What Can Express Love?

They asked Sumnun about love.

Sumnun said:

"One can speak of something
only through something
          more subtle
          and refined.
There is nothing subtler
          than love.
So what
          could ever express
          love?"

SUMNUN

If You Have Lost Heart . . .

If you have lost heart
on the Path of Love

Flee to me
without delay

I am a fortress
invincible

RUMI

Come, Come Again!

Come,
come back!

Repent and come back again
Come!

Come,
whoever you are
infidel
fire worshiper
idol worshiper
Come!

Be not hopeless
in our court

Even if you've broken your vows
a hundred times

Come,
come again!

ABU SAʿID OR BABA AFZAL KASHANI,
COMMONLY ATTRIBUTED TO RUMI

Heaven

Ever since your image
came to call my heart
home

wherever I sit
is
heaven

RUMI

By Any Means Necessary

My precious one

The only obligation in religion
is to arrive at God
by any means necessary

Whatever delivers humanity to God
is an obligation
for the seekers

What delivers the servant to the Lord
is
this love supreme

So
it is love supreme
that is the obligation
of the path to God

ʿAYN AL-QOZAT HAMADANI

Don't Be Meek in This Love

Don't be meek in this love

Be kind to people,
receive the wisdom of the Prophet

but don't be meek in this love
For God is bold
and likes those
who are bold in adoration . . .

This path is for the bold
the intoxicated
the love-crazed

With God
being love-crazed
intoxicated
and bold
works

KHARAQANI

God's Loving Glances

The heart
is nothing but
an ocean of light

The heart
is where
God casts
loving glances

RUMI

This, Too . . .

This
too

shall pass

ʿATTAR

A Short Journey

Choose wholehearted surrender to God
and your journey home

will be
short

KHARAQANI

This Is Love!

Look!
This is love
—to soar toward the heavens

To tear a hundred veils
in every breath
To tear a hundred veils
at the beginning
To travel in the end
without a foot

I said:
"O my heart
may it for you be blessed
To enter
in the circle of the lovers
To look from far beyond
upon
what the eye
cannot see

O soul,
from where comes
this new breath?

O heart,
from where comes
this heavy throbbing?

O bird,
speak now
the language of the birds."

RUMI

Dance in the Light of God

Dance
in the light of God

It's through God
that all from earth to heaven
is made lovely

Every bit of dust
dances
in ecstasy

Dance!

RUMI

God-seer

Not every fragrance
brings the scent of a rose

Not every rock
splits open
gushing water

Not every palm
gives sweet date

Not every bird
finds a home
on the king's arm

Not every heart
becomes a lover

Not every eye
can see God

RUMI

Not Every Eye

Not every down
has an up

Not every eye
has a love-glance

Not every ocean
has a pearl
Not every plant
bears a fruit

Not every king
gives away jewels
Not every sigh
reaches its mark

Not every path
gets to the destination

Not every human
has a heart

Not every cloud
has rain

Wail,
my nightingale!
The lovers' cry
changes the heart
of rocks and thorns

It does

Be like Shams
if you know something
about the heart

Your heart is ready
to journey
in the valley of bewilderment

RUMI

Become Whole

If you are a whole human
See All
Seek All
Become All
Be All
Choose All

'ATTAR

Conforming to God

The female Sufi saint Lubaba was asked about her
preoccupation with God.
She answered:

Intimate knowledge of God
    Bequeaths love for God

Love for God
    Bequeaths longing for God

Longing for God
    Bequeaths intimacy with God

Intimacy with God
    Bequeaths constancy in serving God
    And conforming oneself to God

LUBABA THE WORSHIPER

For the Love of Humanity

Pay attention!

This radical love
is an obligation on the path
for everyone

Take heed:
If you can't attain to the love of the Creator
strive for the love of humanity
so that you can see the worth of these words

'AYN AL-QOZAT

Love as Ascension

Love of a human being
is an ascension
toward love of God
the All-Merciful

RUZBEHAN BAQLI

A Heart No Longer Mine

I lost my heart
somewhere on her face
between her cheek
and the beauty mark

My friends keep asking me
about that beauty
whom I'd worship like an idol

They keep asking
how my heart is doing

How would I know?

It's no longer mine

'AYN AL-QOZAT

A Garden Among the Flames

What wonder is this . . .
a garden among the flames!

My heart takes on every form
a pasture for gazelles,
a cloister for monks,
the idols' temple

A Ka'ba for the circling pilgrim,
the Torah's tables
and the Qur'an's pages

I follow the religion of Love:
Whichever way this caravan turns,
I turn

This love
is my religion,
This,
my faith

IBN 'ARABI

Such Wonders

In this love
spilling over and over
there are
such wonders

'IRAQI

A Cut Diamond

A diamond must be cut
before
its light
can shine out

HAZRAT INAYAT KHAN

Words of Love

I've heard
nothing lovelier
than the melody of love

a keepsake
lingering
in this whirling
azure dome

HAFEZ

Ka'ba and Synagogue

The Ka'ba and synagogue
are the same
to nonbeing

For the shade
heaven and hell
the same

Light cannot burn light

I'm here:

No morning
no night

No fear
no hope

No rank
no station

'IRAQI

God as Love

Radical love
is love
infinite

This is why
it is
a Divine God

RUMI

Friends and Enemies

A thousand friends
are too few

a single enemy
too many

AL-SULAMI

Love Is the GPS

There is no ailment
like the ailment of the heart

Love is the astrolabe
of God's heart secrets

Whether the love you feel
is human
or Divine
ultimately Love
will lead us to God

RUMI

Each of Us Has a Jesus Inside

Every task has a guide that leads humanity onward.

There is a pain, a yearning, a suffering, a love for it that has to
be aroused inside the human, so that we set out to accomplish
it. Without this longing pain for it, no task is accomplished—
whether it is regarding the world, the next world, trade,
imperial rule, knowledge, stars, or whatever else.

Until the birth pangs showed up inside Mary, she didn't aim for
the blessed tree that's mentioned in the Qur'anic verse "The
birth pangs drove her to cling to the trunk of the palm tree." It
was that pain and yearning that led Mary to the tree. A barren
tree became filled with fruit.

Our body is like Mary.
Each of us has a Jesus inside.
If a pain and yearning shows up inside us,
  the Jesus of our soul is born.
If there is no pain, no yearning,
  the Jesus of our soul will return to its origin from the
  same secret passageway that he came from . . .

If there is no pain, no yearning,
we will remain deprived,
not benefiting from that Jesus of the soul.

RUMI

Every Desire Is a Desire for God

Every hope and desire
affection
love
and tenderness
that humanity has

for father
and mother
for brother
and friend
for heaven
and earth
for gardens
and pavilions
for knowledge
and action
for food
and drink

these are all hopes and desires
for God

RUMI

You Are That

You are:
a copy of God's scripture

You are:
mirror of that Regal beauty

Whatever is in the world
is not beyond you

Seek it
inside you

Whatever you seek
you are *that*

RUMI

Many Roads to the Ka'ba

When people hear these words
words that describe God
recalling Him
everyone becomes agitated
they experience God
and yearn for Him

These words carry
the fragrance of the Beloved, the One they seek

There are many paths
The destination is one

Do you not see this?
There are many paths to the Ka'ba
Some come from Byzantium
some from Syria
some from Persia
some from China
some from the sea
some from India and Yemen

If you look at the paths, there is an immense, measureless
    difference among them

But if you look at the destination, everyone comes together.
They are united
inwardly, they have a connection
a love
a great inclination to the Ka'ba
that leaves no room for differences

That attachment is beyond faith and infidelity
That attachment has no connection to the different paths

When they arrived at the Ka'ba
all of their disputation, fighting
and difference of opinion
is laid aside

RUMI

Old Skin

I shed my ego
as a snake discards
its old skin

KHARAQANI

Frenzied Ocean of Love

The ocean's commotion
is because
of yearning
for God

It is the fire of love
that whips
water
into frenzied wave

ʿATTAR

Love Tips the Scale Over

On Resurrection Day,
all of one's deeds will be weighed
on the cosmic scale:
Prayers
Fasting
Charity

Then love will be brought forth
Love doesn't fit
even in that scale

RUMI

A Treasure in Ruins

I make my home
in ruins

How often
the ruin hides
a treasure

'ATTAR

What's All This?

Reason?
gone

Patience?
gone

Beloved?
gone

What is this burning love?
What suffering is this?

What's all this?

'ATTAR

God Breathed with Her

One of God's devotees
had attained to felicity

Hidden from people
she whispered secrets
behind the veil
with God
God was her companion

When she breathed
God breathed

God suffices as a companion

If she were not
and breath were not
God would be enough

ʿATTAR

Secret of Your Heart

You've lost
yourself

Seek the secret
of your heart

Before your soul
departs
seek the secret
of your heart

ʿATTAR

Unafraid

My lips
parched
though I drown
in the ocean

I ask my soul
for the secret
of the Beloved

My only desire
to know the Secret

monsters seek to kill me
I am unafraid

Infidelity and faith both show up
at my heart's door
hand in hand

I open the door
"Welcome!"
"Come inside"

I am unafraid
I know
If God opens the door
Here on the inside
There's neither
infidelity
nor faith

'ATTAR

Waking Up Intoxicated

Rabi'a was staggering one morning, like one who's drunk.
She was asked:

> "What makes you stagger?"

She said:

> "I got intoxicated
> from the love of God last night.
>> His love is making me tipsy."

RABI'A

Heart Awakens

When you enter God's presence
your heart awakens

When you taste love
you'll find
the key
to all the worlds

'ATTAR

What Am I?

I am a lover
I just don't know
whom I love

I'm not a Muslim
not an infidel

What am I?

I am unaware
of this burning love

my heart is filled with it
and empty
all at once

'ATTAR

A Treasure in Every Ruin

Deep
in every ruin
there is a treasure
buried

The buried treasure
in the ruin
of my heart
is your love

RUMI

Your Nothingness

Give to God
your nothingness

He'll give you
His being

KHARAQANI

The Heart's Light

The light
inside the heart's light
is
the light of God

RUMI

LOVER AND BELOVED

A beautiful and perplexing quality of the poetry of the path of radical love is a delicious dance of ambiguity. The seekers of the path of love begin with a realization that love is One, and that love flows from God through humanity and back to God. Therefore the poetry they compose also reflects this journey. In reading mystical love poetry of this tradition, it is hard to determine whether a particular poem is meant for a tender young beloved, for the writer's husband or wife, for a spiritual teacher, for the Prophet Muhammad, or for God.

The truth of the matter is that it is typically written for all of them, and all at once. This ambiguity is a trait of this mingled and mingling radical love, one that unites and unifies the lover and beloved, earth and heaven, male and female, the human and the divine.

As It Shall Be Then

Paradise will be exalted
they say

fine wine
a beautiful beloved

Here and now
we are
intoxicated
cuddling with my beloved

So it is now
as it shall be then

RUMI

Beloved in Embrace, Wine at Hand

A roselike beauty
in my embrace

Wine
at hand

Beloved,
pleased

Next to me
the sultan of the whole world
would be a servant

No need for a candle in this gathering
in our soiree
the beautiful face of my darling
is a full moon

No need for perfume in our banquet
The only fragrance I need
is the musk of your tresses

No need for sugar here
sweetness of your lips
suffices

In our religion wine is permitted
but tonight
it'd be forbidden
without your beautiful face

My ears?
tied to the sound of the flute
and the strumming of the harp

My eyes?
Caught up in your ruby lips
and the sharing of this goblet

Don't talk with me of shame
I've become infamous from this "shame"
why do you speak with me of my name?
I'm ashamed
of whatever name I used to have

We are:
Drunk
head-whirling
rogue
love-glance playing

Who in this whole town isn't like us
like this?

Hafez:
Don't sit for a moment
without wine
and a beloved for the ages

These are the days for roses
and jasmines

Holy days

HAFEZ

Sleepless

Majnun closed his eyes
to sleep
it was only Layla
he saw

I'd be lying if I said
he ever
fell asleep

Where did the morning go?

He tossed and turned all night
till the sun rose

SA ʿ D I

My Beloved

O God!
Publicly I call you
"My Lord"

but in solitude
I call you
"My Beloved"

ABU NUʿAYM ISFAHANI

Mingling

Look:
love mingles with lovers

See:
spirit mingling with body

How long will you see life
as "this"
and "that"?

"Good"
and "bad"?

Look at how this
and that
are mingled

How long will you speak of
"this world"
and "that world"?

See this world
and that world
mingling

RUMI

Love Seeds

We've got nothing to do
except for love

Let's make a vow
you and I

Except for love
and more love
let's plant no seeds
in the pure soil
of our heart

RUMI

Breeze

Breeze:

You hail
from the alley
of that faithful lover

You come
mingled
with a scent
I know so well

The way
you come
caressing me
adding life
to my soul

tells me
all I need to know
about where
you've been

AMIR KHOSROW DEHLAVI

Finding You

I have separated my heart
from this world and its pleasures

My heart and you
are not separate

And when slumber
closes my eyes
I find you
between the eye and the lid

ABU NUʿAYM ISFAHANI

Hundred Ways of Prayer

Today, like every day
we are ruined
ruined

Don't open the door to thought
Pick up a lute instead

For the one prays
toward the Friend's beauty

There are a hundred ways of prayers
Bowing down
And prostration

RUMI

Mine . . . Yours

Three levels of Islam:

First:
> What's mine is mine
> what's yours is yours

Second:
> What's mine is yours
> what's yours is also yours

Third:
> There's neither mine
> nor yours

There is also a fourth level
The rank for lovers

There
there is no longer "me"
nor "you"
> only an Us

ORAL TRADITION, CONTEMPORARY SUFIS

Abode of Demons

Whatever heart
doesn't incline
to love
is not
a heart

It is
the abode
of demons

'IRAQI

My Beloved's Face

Everyone bows
toward the sanctuary
in Mecca

I bow
toward
my beloved's face

ABU SAʿID

A New Love

A new love
comes

The love
that all the loves before
yearned for

I burned

My ashes spelled out
the "No god"
before the "Only God"

To burn yet again
my ashes
came back to life
taking a thousand forms

RUMI

How Can I?

My gracious
flirtatious
beloved

Don't ask me
if I ever think of you

How can I
remember you
When there is no
forgetting you

SA'DI

You Are What You Seek

If you seek jewels in a mine
You are that mine

If you lust after a morsel of bread
You are that piece of bread

Here's a little secret

If you know it
You know it

You are what you seek

RUMI

Same Love

I'll tell you something
amazing
and make it
brief

It's your love
that I'll take
to the grave

the same love
me
will raise

ABU SA'ID

You and I

Faithful friend
come
come closer

Let go
of "you" and "I"

Come
quickly

You and I

have to live

as if
you and I

never heard

of a "you"
and
an "I"

RUMI

Such a Beloved

I have such a beloved
whose love
is inside me

If she so desires
she can trample my cheek
underfoot

HALLAJ

I Fear God . . .

My soul screams out
"what love! What fire!"

This fire
the water of life
is intimate with you

Wish I could borrow a hundred eyes
to keep them all
glancing at you

Where to borrow
such eyes?

Who today casts
such love-glances?

The earth is illuminated
through your face
as if
there are a thousand suns and stars
in the sky

I am ashamed of love
to call you a mere human

I fear God
to call you divine

RUMI

Love Beyond Death

Radical Love is nothing
but heart-shattering grace

Nothing
but the expansion of heart
and guidance

The masters of law
offer no lessons
on love

Religious law is
relevant only until death

Love is for all eternity
infinite

RUMI

Realm of Love

I journeyed to every realm
running here
running there

I have never seen a realm
Like the realm of love
A love that spills over

At the beginning
didn't cherish this love

Not knowing
led me to
an exile of suffering

I let go of this sweet realm
became like an animal
grazing here,
grazing there

Loveless
every sound I heard

was vile
no matter where in the world
I was

A soft voice whispered to me
from the realm of love
"Dear soul,
keep on your journey
it is Me
who created this abode of suffering"

I said:
"I don't want to go
there
into this suffering"

I wailed

He said:
"Go my love
anywhere you like
I am closer to you

than the beating of your heart"

He enchanted me!

This enchantment
I bought with heart and soul

His enchantment
brings the world to dance

Who am I?
Since I returned
to that unmanifest world

I would tell you
that you'll know
when you get here

But the pen broke
when I arrived here

RUMI

Who's Seen Such a Love?

Who's ever seen
such a love
anywhere
in all the worlds

The lovers
plain to see

The Beloved?
Hidden

RUMI

I Need to Go Back

Which way did I come from?

I need to go back
I'm still raw

To be away
from the Friend's alley
in the religion of lovers
is forbidden

RUMI

I'm Yours

I suffer
from myself

Bewildered
In you

If I am good
If I am bad
I'm yours

Without you
I am half
unwhole
look at me!

If you cast
one glance my way
I will be whole

My heart is drenched in blood!

One glance from you
will rescue me

'ATTAR

Tired of Beasts and Demons

Show your face
I yearn for a garden
a rose garden

Open your mouth
I yearn for sweetness

Hold out your hand
I hear the drumbeat
like a falcon
I yearn to land on your arm

Teasing me
You said:
"Torture me no more. Go . . ."
I yearn for you saying
"Torture me no more"

You are a lovely breeze
from the meadow of love
Flow over me
I yearn for the myrtle's scent

I swear this to God
Without you
every realm is a prison to me
I yearn to be distraught
in every plain and desert

On one hand the goblet
the other hand caught
in your tresses
I yearn to dance like this
in the middle
of the lovers' circle

Yesterday a mystic
wandered around the city
with a lit lamp at hand
in broad daylight:

"I'm sick and tired
of beasts and demons!
I yearn for a real human being"

I said to him:
"We've searched
there is none to be found"

He said:
"That one that's not to be found
I yearn for that one—
that one"

RUMI

Pretending to Whisper

In a gathering last night,
saw you

There was a crowd;
couldn't hold you

So I kissed your fragrant hair
a hundred times

Each time pretending
to whisper something
in your ears

ʿAYN AL-QOZAT

I Am Layla

This radical love
is a fire

When it enters a heart
it consumes everything
in the heart

even the Beloved's image
is effaced away
from the heart

Majnun was burning in this love
They told him:
"Layla is coming"

He said:
"I am Layla"

And lowered his head

ʿIRAQI

Be My Layla

Unleash upon me the saga
of being in love
O friend

Be my Layla

For
I am
Majnun

NEZAMI

Hiding Inside My Poems

I'll hide within my poems
as I write them
hoping to kiss your lips
as you recite them

AMAREH

Surrender

All surrender to beauty
willingly
and to power
unwillingly

HAZRAT INAYAT KHAN

Heart Thief

Each day
you come with
a new love
a fresh way

Each time
I look
you get lovelier

I said:
"I'll take you to court
ask for my heart back"

I fear
you'll also steal
the judge's heart

SA'DI

I Wonder

I wonder

this idol
so lovely
cosmos cannot hold her

How does she
make a home
in this lover's heart?

'IRAQI

A Jealous Divine Beloved

The Beloved is jealous in love

He demands that the lover
love no one
other than Him
need no one
other than Him

Therefore, He made Himself into everything
so that whatever the lover loves
Whatever the lover needs
is Him

All this is Him
but is manifest through me

There's no doubt!
It's me
But through Him

'IRAQI

In You

God loves Himself
in you

'IRAQI

Without You

You are my ease
my renewal

You are my life and soul

Without you
I don't breathe well

'IRAQI

I Wish

I am jealous of the earth
upon which you walk

O, I wish instead
that you would walk
on my face
so long as I live

AL-SULAMI

Everything Is Forbidden

It is lovely
for there to be
total informality
between a lover
and a beloved

All these formalities
are for strangers

The only rule is this

Everything is forbidden
except for love

RUMI

Revelation to My Heart

I heard a hidden voice from God
saying
"After Muhammad
We have not sent Gabriel
to any one"

I said
"There is a way
other than Gabriel

God's revelation comes
to my heart
directly"

KHARAQANI

Give Me Back My Heart, Or . . .

Either give me back my heart
or make do with me

Look at my utter need for you
How long will you play
hard to get?
Torture me no more!

If you command it
I'll give my life for you
so that
you bring me back to life
with a kiss on my lips

'ATTAR

Together with a Partner in Paradise

Then I saw my wife in one of the gardens in the presence of
    God (glory be to Him) . . .
in one of the upper chambers of paradise
in the presence of God,
and that upper chamber was of red ruby.

My wife was sitting near the Truth (God) on the side of a
    bench,
as though she was waiting for me.

Then I heard from the voice of the hidden
the saying of the most High,

> *"with the righteous among their parents, and their spouses."*

RUZBEHAN BAQLI

Her Love Slays Me

Her love came
and took me over

Took away my reason
and did with me
whatever she willed

Thoughts of her
lay siege on me
like a highway robber
burning up
all I had harvested

Now without her
I don't breathe well

Being patient without this beloved?
sheer infidelity

Her face
a full moon

Find my path
without her?
Never!

My longing for her?
beyond sickness and remedy

This love
beyond faith and infidelity

This fire in my soul
is from her love

My faith and infidelity?
from her love

Her love
slays me

not a breath longer
will I endure
till I see her

Her love
has thrown me in dust
drowned in blood

The dirt under my feet
will drown in my blood

This is the state of my heart
What am I to do?

'ATTAR

I Seek Her Wherever I Am

A precious soul saw Majnun wrapped up in love's pain.
He was sitting in the middle of the road,
sifting through dirt.

He said:
"O Majnun,
what are you searching for like this?"

Majnun said:
"It's Layla,
of course,
I seek."

He said:
"But where are you going to find Layla
in this dirt?
How can you find a pure pearl
in the dry dirt?"

Majnun said:

"I seek her
wherever I am

Maybe one day
in one breath
   I'll find her"

ʿATTAR

Losing Two

I know
without knowing

I don't know
if you
are I

Or I,
you

I've lost two things:
myself in you
and duality

'ATTAR

She Hushed Me

Last night
in the midst of a crowd

My beloved
adored like an idol
reached over
held me close

in that embrace
She owns all that I am

I said:
"I worship you!"
"I'll *roar* in this love . . ."

She put her lips
on mine
and hushed me

ʿAYN AL-QOZAT

BELOVED
COMMUNITY

The path of radical love is both individual and communal. No one can do the work on our hearts other than we ourselves. We must be the lamps on our own paths. And yet, none of us soars alone. Like the spirit birds in 'Attar's tale *Manteq al-tayr,* we soar together. We need one another as mirrors. It is in others and through others that we see the beauty that is often veiled within ourselves and from ourselves.

To be on the path of radical love is to find God in the very midst of humanity. And one cannot have a Beloved Community without love. It is through this love that we move from the tenderness of interpersonal relationships to justice out in the world. It is through this love that kindness can be actualized, justice can be mobilized, meanness can be neutralized, love can be organized, and the Beloved Community can be realized.

Humanity and Suffering

Humanity are members of one body
Created out of the same essence

when one member of the body
feels pain
others remain distraught

You,
unfeeling to the suffering of others
are unworthy
of the name human

SA'DI

Mirrors

The faithful
is a mirror
for the faithful

HADITH

All of the Path

All of the Path
is beautiful conduct

QUSHAYRI

Togetherness

Togetherness
is mercy

Disunity
is torture

HADITH

Laughing, Crying

You were born
crying

Everyone around you
laughing

Strive to live
so that when you die
you are laughing

and everyone around you
crying

ABU SAʿID

On Saying Farewell to Friends

Whether friends are with you
or away from you
continue loving them

If you part from us,
may God lead you
to beautiful places

When you come to us,
you are always
welcome

When you go,
do not fear
that we will ever
forget you

When you come,
do not feel
that we will ever
have enough of you

YAZID AL-MUHALLABI

Wherever You Are

Wherever you are
be

right
there

fully
present

RUMI

Heart Closed to Humanity

The heart closed
to humanity
means the heart closed
to God

HAZRAT INAYAT KHAN

The Wound Is Where the Light Enters You

Trust your wound
to a skilled healer

You can't see
the ugliness of your own wounds

Flies hover over them:
your thoughts

Your wound is
your heart's state
unilluminated

The healer
this sage
puts a bandage on your wound

The pain
is gone

You think you healed all by yourself
but know this

The healing
was from the light

The wound
is where the light
enters you

RUMI

The Broken-Hearted

God says:

"I am
with those
whose hearts
are
broken"

HADITH QUDSI

Love Someone

You are more
than this beastly form

Humanity
is chivalry
and grace

It's no great skill
to conquer the whole world

If you can
love someone

SA'DI

God Is Manifest

God is manifest
among fellow humans
as the moon shines
       among stars

RUMI

Lord and Servant Leave

When you confess your love
do not expect service

When the lover and beloved enter
Lord and servant leave

SA'DI

A Single Soul

The faithful
are
a single soul

HADITH

Send Thy Peace

Send Thy peace, O Lord,
which is perfect and everlasting
that our souls may radiate peace

Send Thy peace, O Lord,
that we may think, act
and speak harmoniously

Send Thy peace,
O Lord, that we may be contented
and thankful for Thy bountiful gifts

Send Thy peace, O Lord,
that amid our worldly strife
we may enjoy Thy bliss

Send Thy peace, O Lord,
that we may endure all,
tolerate all in the thought of Thy grace and mercy

Send Thy peace, O Lord,
that our lives may become a divine vision
and in Thy light all darkness may vanish

Send Thy peace, O Lord,
our Father and Mother
that we Thy children on earth may all unite in one family
Amen.

HAZRAT INAYAT KHAN

Perfection of Love, Harmony, and Beauty

Toward the One
the Perfection of Love, Harmony, and Beauty
the Only Being
united with all the Illuminated Souls
who form the Embodiment of the Master
the Spirit of Guidance

HAZRAT INAYAT KHAN

Bless All That We Receive

O Thou
the Sustainer of our bodies,
hearts
and souls

Bless all that we receive
in thankfulness

HAZRAT INAYAT KHAN

Do Not Run After

Receive the one
who comes

Do not run
after the one
who turns his back on you

AL-SULAMI

Digging a Hole

If you dig a hole
for your brother
to fall in

you yourself
will fall in it

HADITH

Forget All the Good

Know the value of your friends
and in their company
      forget all the good deeds
you did for them

AL-SULAMI

As Above, So Below

The merciful ones
will be shown mercy
by the All-Merciful

Be merciful
to those on Earth
and the One in Heaven
will be merciful to you

HADITH

Never Leave Your Friends

Show your continuous love
and understanding
and never leave your friends
because of the inconvenience
they may cause

AL-SULAMI

Let Us Reconcile!

Come
Let's cherish each other

Let us live
attuned to each other

Enmity takes the light
out of friendship

Let's banish all enmity
from our hearts

Does it bring joy to your heart
to imagine me dead?

Why are we like this?
worshiping death
hating life?

If I die
You'll want to make up

Pretend I'm dead now
Come,
let's reconcile our hearts now

In submitting to God
our egos have already died

If I die
you'll come to kiss my grave

We are now like this

Come
now
and kiss my face

RUMI

Response to Love

Love
must be met
by love

The only proper response
to love
is love

AL-SULAMI

Soft as Soil

How can spring flowers
grow on stones?

Be soft
Like the soil

So colorful roses
grow inside

For years
you've had a heart of stone

Try for a while
being soft
as soil

RUMI

As Long As

As long as I see him
I do not care to see anything else

As long as I hear his words
I do not care to hear anyone else

AL-SULAMI

Living Away from Loved Ones

After suffering the pangs of love
I have no place to go

How empty it is
when the beloved is gone

To live away from those whom we love
is not living at all

AL-SULAMI

The Real Ka'ba

What is meant by the Ka'ba
is the heart
of the prophets
and the friends of God

That
is where God is revealed

RUMI

Serve Your Mother

Once there were two brothers, who lived with their mother.

Every night one brother would devote himself to serving the
    mother,
whereas the other brother occupied himself with worshiping
    God.

One night the brother who worshiped God had a dream, in
    which he heard a voice from Beyond telling him:

"We have forgiven your brother,
and for his sake, have forgiven you as well."

The brother said: "But I have occupied myself with worshiping
    God,
whereas he has occupied himself with serving our mother.
You are forgiving me for his sake?"

He heard the voice of God say:

"That which you do for me, I have no need for.
But your mother needs the service your brother provides."

KHARAQANI

These Do Not Matter

Come to the orchard in the Spring
There is light and wine
and sweethearts in the pomegranate flowers

If you do not come
these do not matter

If you do come
these do not matter

RUMI

Judge Not

Judge
not

Hold
your tongue

Avoid
fanaticism

Make the path
your only purpose

'ATTAR

Accept Without Blame

A female Sufi, Mu'adha, was asked about how to live in accordance with the words of God "*forgive with a beautiful forgiveness.*"

> She answered:
> "*Be content.*
> *Accept people without assigning blame.*"

MU'ADHA UMM AL-ASWAD

Idol Maker

If being praised and blamed
makes a difference to you
you are nothing
but an idol maker

If you still have a hundred idols
hidden inside your robe

Why do you pretend to be
a Sufi
in front of people?

'ATTAR

Loving the Artist

'Aisha, the daughter of Abu 'Uthman, was asked about the need to show beautiful conduct toward humanity.

She answered:

> *Who loves the Artist*
> *glorifies the art*

'AISHA, THE DAUGHTER OF ABU 'UTHMAN

A Raging Hellfire

It is unwise
to remain with your ego

Know this:

Your ego is
a raging hellfire

'ATTAR

Give It Away

Whatever you have
give it away

here
there
everywhere

The Qur'an says:
*"You won't attain to good
until you freely give away
what you love."*

You have to give away
everything

Even
your soul

That too
must be given away

'ATTAR

Every Breath Is a Jewel

Every breath
each breath
of your life
is a precious jewel

Every new atom
guides you
toward God

How patient you've become
being apart from Him

God has raised you
with a hundred glories
and loving games

You don't know this!
and keep thinking of yourself
as other than Him

ʿATTAR

Idols Inside

Smashing idols outside
is easy
so easy

Seeing your own ego
as an idol?

Hard
so hard

You want to know the tale
of your ego
my child?

Think of hellfire
with seven gates

RUMI

What's Your Puddle of Piss?

A fly sat
on a straw
on a puddle of donkey piss

full of pride
it lifted up its head:

"I am the captain of this ship
master of this ocean!"

RUMI

Our Brokenness

You're clutching
with both hands

to this myth
of "you" and "I"

our whole brokenness
is because of this

RUMI

Remove the Ka'ba

God commands us
to pray in the direction of the Ka'ba

Imagine this:
People all over the world
are gathered
making a circle
around the Ka'ba

They bow down
in prayer

Now
imagine:

Remove the Ka'ba
from the middle of the circle

Are they not prostrating
toward one another?

They are bowing down
toward each other's hearts

SHAMS-E TABRIZI

Don't Blame the Night

The night has ended
Our tale has not

Don't blame the night

Our love story
takes too long

RUMI

God Remains

These words of intoxication come to me

Forgive me!

No choice
Have I
fallen into an ocean
Without shore

I rival the seven seas
Though I haven't the strength
For a single dewdrop

There is no room
For hopelessness

My heart swims
In an ocean of hope

My tired soul,
arriving at the shore,
cries out:

How can we
Be apart from us?

You and I
Departed

God remains

ʿIRAQI

Sources

Unless otherwise indicated, all translations are mine.

God of Love

"Whichever Way You Turn," Qur'an 2:115.

"One Love," Qur'an 5:54.

"Not This, Not That. Both This and That," Ahmad Ghazali, *Sawanih,* 3.

"The Opening," Qur'an 1:1–7. Translation by Bilal Hyde. I have modified the translation by rendering "Allah" as "God." The exclamation at the end, *Amin,* is from the same root as *Amen* in English. In Arabic, it contains the root of finding safety and security in God's presence.

"Love and Justice," Qur'an 16:90. The word translated here as "love" is *Ihsan,* the highest quality of faith of making beauty real here and now. It refers to the whole realm of love, mercy, and beauty that is the pinnacle of the relationship with God, nature, and the human community.

"A God Closer Than . . .," Qur'an 50:16.

"God Intervenes," Qur'an 8:24.

"Signs of God," Qur'an 41:53.

"Enter Inside My Servants," Qur'an 89:27.

"Remembrance of God," Qur'an 13:28.

"Never Give Up Hope," Qur'an 39:53. The Prophet Muhammad says, in the hadith collection of Tirmidhi, that he loves this verse of the Qur'an more than the entire world, and all there is within the world.

"Face of God," Qur'an 55:26–27.

"Wherever," Qur'an 57:4.

"Where Is God?" The hadith cited here is from 'Ayn al-Qozat, *Tamhidat*, 148.

"Muhammad as Mercy," Qur'an 21:107.

"Perfect Our Light," Qur'an 66:8.

"God's Mercy," Hadith Qudsi. The Hadith Qudsi are a privileged non-Qur'anic genre of communication directly between Muhammad and God. They often reveal the intimacies between humanity and the divine. There is no canonical collection of Hadith Qudsi, and they are frequently cited in many classic works of Sufism. This particular Hadith Qudsi is found in the hadith collection by the scholar named Muslim, and is recorded in *Forty Hadith Qudsi*, selected and translated by Ezzeddin Ibrahim and Denys Johnson-Davies, 40–41. Cf. Rumi, *Masnavi*, 1:2672.

"Hidden Treasure," Hadith Qudsi. Recorded in Badi' al-Zaman Foruzanfar, *Ahadis va Qesas-e Masnavi*, 120.

"God, Love, and Beauty," hadith, recorded in the collection by the scholar Muslim. Also see Rumi, *Masnavi*, 2:79, and Ruzbehan Baqli, *Abhar al-'ashiqin*, 31.

"Show Mercy," hadith collection of Termezi [Arabic: Tirmidhi]. Recorded in Badi' al-Zaman Foruzanfar, *Ahadis va Qesas-e Masnavi*, 35–36.

"For the Sake of Muhammad," Hadith Qudsi. This version is cited in Rumi, *Fihi ma fihi,* chapter 54, p. 193, and *Masnavi,* 5:2537. Cf. Badiʿ al-Zaman Foruzanfar, *Ahadis va Qesas-e Masnavi,* 484. Another version of the same hadith reads as:

"If Muhammad had not been, I would not have created this world and the Hereafter,

the Heavens and the Earth, the Throne, the Tablet and the Pen, the Garden and the Fire. Were it not for Muhammad, I would not have created at all."

"A Heart to Contain God," Hadith Qudsi. This version is cited in Rumi, *Masnavi,* 1:3071–73.

"Uninterrupted Lightning," Qushayri's *Risala,* chapter titled "Muhadara, Mukashafa, Mushahada," quoting ʿAmr ibn ʿUthman al-Makki. Cf. *Al-Qushayri's Epistle on Sufism (al-Risala al-Qushayriyya fi ʿilm al-tasawwuf),* translated by Alexander Knysh, 98.

"A Moment," hadith. Cf. Rumi, *Masnavi,* 1:3953, Badiʿ al-Zaman Foruzanfar, *Ahadis va Qesas-e Masnavi,* 152.

"Know Thyself," Hadith Qudsi. This version is cited in Rumi, *Masnavi,* 4:547.

"God Sees Your Hearts," hadith. Cited in the biography of the saint by Ebn Monavvar [Arabic: Ibn Munawwar], *Asrar al-Tawhid,* 1:86. In Persian references, Abu Saʿid ibn Abi ʾl-Khayr is often referred to as Abu Saʿid-e Abi ʾl-Khayr. Also in ʿAttar, "Rabiʿa," *Tazkerat al-awliya',* 72.

"Lord of the Kaʿba," ʿAttar, *Tazkerat al-awliya',* 75.

"Removing Dirt from the Path," in Ebn Monavvar, *Asrar al-Tawhid,* 1:205.

"Divine Qualities," Hadith Qudsi. Cited in 'Ayn al-Qozat, *Tamhidat,* 129. A more literal translation would be: "Qualify yourself with divine qualities."

"Beloved So Close to Me," Sa'di, *Golestan* (Rose Garden), 319.

"Be at Ease," quoted in 'Attar, *Tazkerat al-awliya',* "Sahl ibn 'Abd-Allah al-Tostari," 317.

"The Heart of Your Friend," Khwaja 'Abdullah Ansari, *Monajat.*

"Something Else," Sabri Brothers, Qawwali song, *Ya Mohammad, Nur-e Mojassam,* "O Muhammad, Light Embodied."

"Saying 'I,'" Abu Bakr Kharraz. Quoted in Annemarie Schimmel, *Mystical Dimensions of Islam,* 55. This idea has a long legacy in Islamic thought, going back to the sixth Shi'i Imam Ja'far Sadiq, and also Hallaj and al-Wasiti. See Carl Ernst, *Words of Ecstasy in Sufism,* 10; Laury Silvers, *Soaring Minaret,* 47.

"Forgiveness," Hafez, *Divan-e Hafez* (Khanlari edition), *Ghazal* 279, 574.

"You Are Greater," al-Sulami, *The Way of Sufi Chivalry,* 105.

"God in Search of Humanity," Hadith Qudsi, transmitted through Companion of the Prophet, Ka'b al-Ahbar, cited in Ebn Monavvar, *Asrar al-Tawhid,* "Secrets of God's Unity," 1:243.

"A Single Breath," 'Attar.

"It's All Him!" 'Attar, *Manteq al-tayr,* 7–8, lines 127–31.

"Muhammad, the Maternal Prophet," 'Attar, *Tazkerat al-awliya'*, 22, ll. 414–18.

One of the honorifics of the Prophet is *Ummi*, which usually gets translated as the Unlettered Prophet, meaning that the Prophet's knowledge does not come from mere human learning. Some of the Sufis, however, playfully picked up on the idea that Ummi also comes from the root word *Umm*, which means mother. In other words, Muhammad is also the maternal prophet, the prophet who loves the community the way a mother does. In this poem 'Attar is asking the maternal prophet to suckle him, and the community, through the breast of compassion and generosity. This desire to have an intimate, bodily connection with the Prophet was not uncommon among the radical love mystics.

"At Last," Hazrat Inayat Khan, *Gayan*, 54–55.

"Heart, Lord," Abu 'l-Husayn al-Nuri, cited by Qushayri, *Risala*. Cf. *Al-Qushayri's Epistle on Sufism (al-Risala al-Qushayriyya fi 'ilm al-tasawwuf)*, translated by Alexander Knysh, 84.

"No Way to Treat a Friend," Rabi'a in 'Attar, *Tazkerat al-awliya'*, 87.

"Forgive Freely!" Khwaja 'Abd Allah Ansari, *Monajat*, 26. The original reads "merchant" in place of "accountant," but in English *accountant* has more the connotation implied here of one who rules by justice and measurement of good deeds, as opposed to mercy.

"God's Path," Fakhr al-Din 'Iraqi, *Lama'at*, chapter 15, p. 494.

"Love, Harmony, and Beauty," Hazrat Inayat Khan, *Gayan*, 45.

"Prayer of Rabi'a," in 'Attar, *Tazkerat al-awliya'*, 87.

"This and That," Fakhr al-Din 'Iraqi, *Lama'at*, chapter 13, p. 490.

"Lord of the Path," in Ebn Monavvar, *Asrar al-Tawhid*, 1:259.

"No Heaven, No Hell," in 'Attar, "Abu 'l-Hasan Kharaqani," *Tazkerat al-awliya'*, 682.

"But I Know," 'Attar, *Manteq al-tayr*, pp. 102–3, ll. 1841–59.

"Seeing Nothing Other than God," Sa'di, *Qasa'ed-e Sa'di*, edited by Muhammad Ali Foruqi, 98; also Sa'di, *Kolliyat*, 789.

"God's Not Lost," 'Attar, *Manteq al-tayr*, p. 182, l. 3272.

"My Only Shame," Qa'ani. Qa'ani was a nineteenth-century Persian poet, the first Persian poet familiar with Western languages.

"Door Never Closed," in 'Attar, *Manteq al-tayr*, p. 186, ll. 3331–32. Also see Arabic text in Rkia E. Cornell, *Early Sufi Women*, 81.

"A Deal with God," in 'Attar, "Abu 'l-Hasan Kharaqani," *Tazkerat al-awliya'*, 672.

"Where Do You See God?" in 'Attar, "Abu 'l-Hasan Kharaqani," *Tazkerat al-awliya'*, 691.

"My Only Need," Rayhana "the Enraptured," in al-Sulami's *Dhikr al-muta'abbidat al-sufiyyat*. Arabic text in Rkia E. Cornell, *Early Sufi Women*, 95.

"Seeing God," in 'Attar, "Abu 'l-Hasan Kharaqani," *Tazkerat al-awliya'*, 704.

"God's Lap," quoted in Qushayri, *Risala*. Chapter titled "Tasawwuf/ Sufism." Cf. *Al-Qushayri's Epistle on Sufism (al-Risala al-Qushayriyya fi 'ilm al-tasawwuf)*, translated by Alexander Knysh, 291.

"Everywhere You Look," in 'Attar, "Abu 'l-Hasan Kharaqani,"
Tazkerat al-awliya', 706.

"Finding God," in 'Attar, "Abu 'l-Hasan Kharaqani," *Tazkerat
al-awliya'*, 709.

Path of Love

"Say Nothing," Rumi, *Divan-e Shams,* Ghazal 2219, 5:65.

"Muhammad on Perfume, Women, and Prayer," Hadith of the
Prophet, cited in Ibn 'Arabi's *Fusus al-hikam.* Muhammad spoke
about the sensual pleasures of this world (symbolized by perfume)
and the realm of love (exemplified through love shared between men
and women) as leading one to God. Some commentators have
reflected on the fact that Muhammad speaks of "being made to love"
these three, to reflect that it is not his own desire, but a love for them
that God has placed in his heart.

"Water Takes on the Color of the Cup," Fakhr al-Din 'Iraqi,
Lama'at, chapter 5, p. 469.

"Many Paths to the Ka'ba," Rumi, *Fihi Ma Fihi,* chapter 23, p. 90.

"Pain," Rumi, *Masnavi,* 1:2980.

"Looking for God in Hearts," Rumi, *Masnavi,* 1:2653–55. Cf.
Badi' al-Zaman Foruzanfar, *Ahadis va Qesas-e Masnavi,* 113. Rumi is
paraphrasing a Hadith Qudsi here.

"A Love Beyond Time," Rumi, *Masnavi,* 1:1759.

"Accept Whatever Comes from God," Rumi, *Masnavi,* 1:1764.

"Everything Sings," in Ebn Monavvar, *Asrar al-Tawhid,* 1:130.

"An Awake Heart," hadith in the collection of Bukhari. Also see Rumi, *Masnavi,* 2:3549–50.

"Martyr of Love," hadith from the Prophet Muhammad; recorded in 'Ayn al-Qozat, *Tamhidat,* 96. Also cited in Fakhr al-Din 'Iraqi, *Lama'at,* chapter 7, p. 475.

"Mi'raj," Rumi, *Divan-e Shams,* Ghazal 133, 1:87.

"I Want Not to Want," Sa'di, *Golestan* (Rose Garden), 424.

"Nothing Owns You," Abu Nasr al-Sarraj, *Kitab al-Luma',* 25.

"Joy Inside the Heart," Rumi, *Masnavi,* 3:3260.

"Ocean of Sorrow," Rumi, *Masnavi,* 2:1771.

"A Blazing Lightning," Shebli, quoted in Qushayri, *Risala.* Cf. *Al-Qushayri's Epistle on Sufism (al-Risala al-Qushayriyya fi 'ilm al-tasawwuf),* translated by Alexander Knysh, 291.

"Leaping Heavenward," Rumi, *Divan-e Shams,* Ghazal 463, 1:269–70. Also see Aflaki, *Manaqeb al-'Arefin,* 1:266.

"A Secret," Rumi, *Divan-e Shams,* Quatrain 78.

"Wordless Secrets," Rumi, *Divan-e Shams,* Ghazal 296, 1:180.

"Endless Beloved," in 'Attar, "Zol-Nun" [Arabic: Dhu 'l-Nun], *Tazkerat al-awliya',* 1:123.

"Sound of One-Handed Clapping," Rumi, *Masnavi,* 3:4392–97.

"Power of the Words of Love," in 'Attar, *Tazkerat al-awliya',* 511–12.

"What Can Express Love?" in 'Attar, *Tazkerat al-awliya',* 513.

"If You Have Lost Heart . . .," Rumi, *Divan-e Shams.* Translation is from William Chittick, *The Sufi Path of Love: Spiritual Teachings of Rumi,* i.

"Come, Come Again!" This well-known quatrain is often, and mistakenly, attributed to Rumi. It is probably from Abu Sa'id-e Abi 'l-Khayr (Ruba'i 1) or from Rumi's contemporary Baba Afzal Kashani. See Ibrahim Gamard and Farhan Ravadi, *The Quatrains of Rumi,* 609, where the misattribution is blamed on the late Ottoman Necati Bey.

"Heaven," Rumi, *Divan-e Shams,* Ghazal 644, 2:63. The word *Baz* has multiple meanings: again (as in "come back, again"), falcon ("take to flight like a falcon"), and open (as in an "open heart"). I have tried to convey all of these meanings here.

"By Any Means Necessary," 'Ayn al-Qozat Hamadani [Arabic: 'Ayn al-Qudat al-Hamadhani], *Tamhidat,* 97.

"Don't Be Meek in This Love," Kharaqani. Modified from Vraje Abramian, *The Soul and A Loaf of Bread: The Teachings of Sheikh Abol-Hasan of Kharaqan,* 4. The original is from Mohammadreza Shafi'i-Kadkani, *Neveshteh Bar Darya,* 211.

"God's Loving Glances," Rumi, *Masnavi,* 3:2269.

"This, Too . . .," 'Attar, *Elahi-nama.* Omid Safi, "'Attar, Farid al-Din," *Encyclopedia of Islam.*

"A Short Journey," Kharaqani. Modified from Vraje Abramian, *The Soul and A Loaf of Bread: The Teachings of Sheikh Abol-Hasan of Kharaqan,* 9. The original is from Mohammadreza Shafi'i-Kadkani, *Neveshteh Bar Darya,* 49, and reads "Choose the path of certainty."

"This Is Love!" Rumi, *Divan-e Shams,* Ghazal 1919, 4:177. Translated by Annemarie Schimmel, translation modified.

"Dance in the Light of God," Rumi, *Divan-e Shams* (Jalal al-Din Homa'i edition, p. 184). The Foruzanfar edition of *Divan-e Shams* (1:297, Ghazal 510) reads slightly differently, "Dance in the light of the Intellect," *Nur-e kherad* instead of *Nur-e khoda.* But even there the previous lines refer to "the light of God that brings every footless particle to ecstatic foot-stomping dance!"

"God-seer," Rumi, *Divan-e Shams,* Jalal al-Din Homa'i edition, 189.

"Not Every Eye," blending together two slight variants in Rumi, *Divan-e Shams* (Jalal al-Din Homa'i edition), 222, and Rumi, *Divan-e Shams,* Ghazal 563, 2:22.

"Become Whole," 'Attar, *Manteq al-tayr,* p. 47, l. 839.

"Conforming to God," in al-Sulami, *Dhikr al-muta'abbidat al-sufiyyat.* Translation modified from Rkia E. Cornell, *Early Sufi Women,* 124–25.

"For the Love of Humanity," 'Ayn al-Qozat, *Tamhidat,* 96.

"Love as Ascension," Ruzbehan Baqli, *'Abhar al-ashiqin,* 88.

"A Heart No Longer Mine," 'Ayn al-Qozat, *Tamhidat,* 117.

"A Garden Among the Flames," Ibn 'Arabi, *Tarjuman al-Ashwaq.* Translated by Omid Safi from the Arabic original, based on the translation offered by Reynold A. Nicholson in *The Tarjuman al-Ashwaq: A Collection of Mystical Odes by Muhyi'ddin Ibn al-'Arabi.* Edited and translated by Nicholson, 19. I am also grateful to Michael Sells, who has offered a superb translation of the same poem in his *Mystical Language of Unsaying,* 90.

"Such Wonders," Fakhr al-Din 'Iraqi, *Lama'at,* chapter 6, p. 472.

"A Cut Diamond," Hazrat Inayat Khan, *Gayan,* 17.

"Words of Love," Hafez, *Divan-e-Hafez* (Khanlari edition), Ghazal 175, 366.

"Ka'ba and Synagogue," Fakhr al-Din 'Iraqi, *Lama'at,* chapter 10, p. 484.

"God as Love," Rumi, *Masnavi,* introduction to volume 2, p. 181.

"Friends and Enemies," al-Sulami, *The Way of Sufi Chivalry,* 92.

"Love Is the GPS," Rumi, *Masnavi,* 1:109–11. The astrolabe was a medieval device that was perfected by Muslim astronomers. It was used to find one's way on sea and land, a premodern GPS device. The analogy is profound: we as humanity are "lost."

We need to orient ourselves to God to find our way home. What takes us home is radical love. Love is the "Go Home" option to take us back to God, at once our home, the path, and the destination.

"Each of Us Has a Jesus Inside," Rumi, *Fihi ma fihi,* chapter 5, p. 18–19.

"Every Desire Is a Desire for God," Rumi, *Fihi ma fihi,* chapter 9, p. 32.

"You Are That," Rumi, *Fihi ma fihi,* chapter 16, p. 70. Ibrahim Gamard and Rawan Farhadi, *The Quatrains of Rumi,* p. 600, discuss whether the same poem could have belonged to Awhad al-Din Kermani or Najm al-Din Razi.

"Many Roads to the Ka'ba," Rumi, *Fihi ma fihi*, chapter 23, p. 90.

"Old Skin," in 'Attar, "Abu 'l-Hasan Kharaqani," *Tazkerat al-awliya'*, 684.

"Frenzied Ocean of Love," 'Attar, *Manteq al-tayr*, p. 56, ll. 1000–1002.

"Love Tips the Scale Over," Rumi, *Fihi ma fihi*, chapter 59, p. 205. Rumi is alluding to the notion that in the Hereafter, the good deeds of each individual will be measured against his/her evil deeds, and then treated with both divine justice and mercy. In this reckoning, Rumi opines that once all the righteous religious deeds have been accounted for, then love is brought forth that will tip the scale toward the good and beautiful. This love, like all radical love, is both the love that we as human beings have expressed and God's love.

"A Treasure in Ruins," 'Attar, *Manteq al-tayr*, p. 57, l. 1009.

"What's All This?" 'Attar, *Manteq al-tayr*, p. 71, l. 1267.

"God Breathed with Her," 'Attar, *Manteq al-tayr*, p. 119, ll. 2134–36.

"Secret of Your Heart," 'Attar, *Manteq al-tayr*, p. 132, l. 2380.

"Unafraid," 'Attar, *Manteq al-tayr*, p. 181, ll. 2346–49.

"Waking Up Intoxicated," Rabi'a al-'Adawiyya, in al-Sulami's *Dhikr al-muta'abbidat al-sufiyyat*. Arabic text in Rkia E. Cornell, *Early Sufi Women*, 79. Translation modified.

"Heart Awakens," 'Attar, *Manteq al-tayr*, p. 198, ll. 3552, 3557.

"What Am I?" 'Attar, *Manteq al-tayr*, p. 212, ll. 3812–13.

"A Treasure in Every Ruin," Rumi, *Divan-e Shams*, Ruba'iyyat 1488, 8:251.

"Your Nothingness," in 'Attar, "Abu 'l-Hasan Kharaqani," *Tazkerat al-awliya*, 701.

"The Heart's Light," Rumi, *Masnavi* 1:1127.

Lover and Beloved

"As It Shall Be Then," Rumi, *Divan-e Shams*, Quatrain 755, 8:128.

"Beloved in Embrace, Wine at Hand," Hafez, *Divan-e Hafez* (Khanlari edition), Ghazal 47, 110.

"Sleepless," Sa'di, *Kolliyat-e Sa'di* (Foruqi edition), Ghazal 213, 505.

"My Beloved," Abu Nu'aym Isfahani, *Hilyat al-awliya*, 9:332.

"Mingling," Rumi, *Divan-e Shams*, Ghazal 2381, 5:157.

"Love Seeds," Rumi, *Divan-e Shams*, Ghazal 1475, 3:224.

"Breeze," Amir Khosrow Dehlavi, *Divan*, Ghazal 625.

"Finding You," Abu Nu'aym Isfahani, *Hilyat al-awliya*, 10:310.

"Hundred Ways of Prayer," Rumi, *Divan-e Shams*, Ruba'iyyat 81, 8:14.

"Mine . . . Yours," oral tradition, contemporary Sufis.

"Abode of Demons," Fakhr al-Din 'Iraqi, *Dah Fasl*, 406.

"My Beloved's Face," in Ebn Monavvar, *Asrar al-Tawhid*, 1:53.

"A New Love," Rumi, *Divan-e Shams*, Quatrain 598, 8:102.

"How Can I?" Sa'di, *Kolliyat-e Sa'di* (Foruqi edition), Ghazal 535, 670.

"You Are What You Seek," Rumi, *Divan-e Shams,* Quatrain 1875.

"Same Love," Abu Sa'id. Persian original is in Dick Davis, *Borrowed Ware,* 56. Translation is my own.

"You and I," Rumi, *Divan-e Shams,* Ghazal 251, 1:157.

"Such a Beloved," Hallaj, recited by Abed Azrie on the CD *Aromates.*

"I Fear God . . .," Rumi, *Divan-e Shams,* Ghazal 450, 1:261.

"Love Beyond Death," Rumi, *Divan-e Shams,* 209.

"Realm of Love," Rumi, *Divan-e Shams,* Ghazal 1509, 3:242–43.

"Who's Seen Such a Love?" Rumi, *Divan-e Shams,* Ghazal 824, 2:160.

"I Need to Go Back," Rumi, *Divan-e Shams,* 185. The Friend (*doost*) in the language of Radical Love mystics can refer simultaneously to a human or a Divine Beloved.

"I'm Yours," 'Attar, *Manteq al-tayr,* p. 13, ll. 240–42.

"Tired of Beasts and Demons," Rumi, *Divan-e Shams,* 203–4.

"Pretending to Whisper," 'Ayn al-Qozat, *Tamhidat,* 278.

"I Am Layla," Fakhr al-Din 'Iraqi, *Lama'at,* chapter 23, pp. 518–19.

"Be My Layla," Nezami, *Divan.* Published in *The Story of Layla and Majnun.* Translated from Persian and edited by Dr. Rudolf Gelpke. Final chapter (and this poem) translated from the Persian by Zia Inayat Khan and Omid Safi.

"Hiding Inside My Poems," Amareh. Recited by Abu Sa'id-e Abi 'l-Khayr in a mystical session of music and poetry. Source is Ebn Monavvar, *Asrar al-Tawhid,* "Secrets of God's Unity," 1:267. Translation is from Davis, *Borrowed Ware,* 55.

"Surrender," Hazrat Inayat Khan, *Gayan,* 21.

"Heart Thief," Sa'di, Quatrains. *Kolliyat-e Sa'di* (Foruqi edition), 759.

"I Wonder," Fakhr al-Din 'Iraqi, *Lama'at,* chapter 19, p. 508. Another manuscript ("L") reads: "in my anguished heart."

"A Jealous Divine Beloved," Fakhr al-Din 'Iraqi, *Lama'at,* chapter 4, p. 464.

"In You," Fakhr al-Din 'Iraqi, *Lama'at,* chapter 4, p. 465.

"Without You," paraphrased from William Chittick's introduction to *Divine Flashes [Lama'at],* 51.

"I Wish," al-Sulami, *The Way of Sufi Chivalry,* p. 85.

"Everything Is Forbidden," Rumi, *Fihi ma fihi,* chapter 20, p. 82.

"Revelation to My Heart," in 'Attar, "Abu 'l-Hasan Kharaqani," *Tazkerat al-awliya',* 672.

"Give Me Back My Heart, Or . . .," 'Attar, *Manteq al-tayr,* p. 74, ll. 1313, 1316.

"Together with a Partner in Paradise," Ruzbehan Baqli, *Kashf al-asrar.* Translation is by Carl W. Ernst, from *Unveiling of Secrets: Diary of a Sufi Master,* 54.

"Her Love Slays Me," 'Attar, *Manteq al-tayr,* p. 124, ll. 2221–31.

"I Seek Her Wherever I Am," 'Attar, *Manteq al-tayr,* p. 183, ll. 3288–91.

"Losing Two," 'Attar, *Manteq al-tayr,* p. 209, ll. 3751–52.

"She Hushed Me," 'Ayn al-Qozat, *Tamhidat,* p. 128.

Beloved Community

"Humanity and Suffering," Sa'di, *Golestan* (Rose Garden), 190.

"Mirrors," hadith, cited in Rumi, *Masnavi,* 2:30.

"All of the Path," Qushayri, *Risala. Al-Qushayri's Epistle on Sufism (al-Risala al-Qushayriyya fi 'ilm al-tasawwuf),* translated by Alexander Knysh, 290.

"Togetherness," hadith. Rumi, *Masnavi,* 1:3017; Cf. Badi' al-Zaman Foruzanfar, *Ahadis va Qesas-e Masnavi,* 128.

"Laughing, Crying," in Ebn Monavvar, *Asrar al-Tawhid,* "Secrets of God's Unity," 1:243.

"On Saying Farewell to Friends," Yazid al-Muhallabi, cited in al-Sulami, *The Way of Sufi Chivalry,* 95, modified.

"Wherever You Are," Rumi, *Divan-e Shams,* Ghazal 1377, 3:172.

"Heart Closed to Humanity," Hazrat Inayat Khan, *Gayan,* 16. Language slightly modified.

"The Wound Is Where the Light Enters You," Rumi, *Masnavi,* 1:3222–27.

"The Broken-Hearted," Hadith Qudsi. The full version of the saying states: "I am with those whose hearts are broken for My sake." Rumi, *Masnavi,* 1:532, cites the shorter version represented indicated here. Recorded in Badi' al-Zaman Foruzanfar, *Ahadis va Qesas-e*

Masnavi, 28. Also cited by Ibn 'Arabi in *Futuhat al-Makiyya.* See William Chittick, *The Self-Disclosure of God,* 395.

"Love Someone," Sa'di, *Golestan* (Rose Garden), 590. Literally: "win over a heart."

"God Is Manifest," Rumi, *Masnavi,* 1:1400, 70. Literally "among others."

"Lord and Servant Leave," Sa'di, *Golestan* (Rose Garden), 507.

"A Single Soul," hadith. Cf. Badi' al-Zaman Foruzanfar, *Ahadis va Qesas-e Masnavi,* 159; Rumi, *Masnavi,* 2:188.

"Send Thy Peace," attributed to Hazrat Inayat Khan, "Prayer for Peace." I am grateful to Pir Zia Inayat Khan for confirming the origin of this poem in *Sufi* magazine, July 1918, vol. 3, no. 2.

"Perfection of Love, Harmony, and Beauty," Hazrat Inayat Khan.

"Bless All That We Receive," Hazrat Inayat Khan, *Gayan,* 48.

"Do Not Run After," al-Sulami, *The Way of Sufi Chivalry,* 60.

"Digging a Hole," Hadith. Rumi, *Masnavi,* 1:1311. Cf. Badi' al-Zaman Foruzanfar, *Ahadis va Qesas-e Masnavi,* 62.

"Forget All the Good," al-Sulami, *The Way of Sufi Chivalry,* 76.

"As Above, So Below," Hadith Tirmidhi.

"Never Leave Your Friends," al-Sulami, *The Way of Sufi Chivalry,* 82.

"Let Us Reconcile!" Rumi, *Divan-e Shams,* Ghazal 1535, 3:256.

"Response to Love," al-Sulami, *The Way of Sufi Chivalry,* 85.

"Soft as Soil," Rumi, *Masnavi,* 1:1911–12, 91.

"As Long As," al-Sulami, *The Way of Sufi Chivalry,* 86.

"Living Away from Loved Ones," al-Sulami, *The Way of Sufi Chivalry,* 93.

"The Real Ka'ba," Rumi, *Fihi ma fihi,* chapter 43, 156.

"Serve Your Mother," in 'Attar, "Abu 'l-Hasan Kharaqani," *Tazkerat al-awliya',* 671.

"These Do Not Matter," Rumi, *Divan-e Shams,* Quatrain 888, 8:150, translated by Coleman Barks, *Open Secret,* 14. Used with permission from Coleman Barks.

"Judge Not," 'Attar, *Manteq al-tayr,* p. 34, l. 605.

"Accept Without Blame," Mu'adha Umm al-Aswad, in al-Sulami, *Dhikr al-muta'abbidat al-sufiyyat.* Arabic text in Rkia E. Cornell, *Early Sufi Women,* 105. Translation modified.

"Idol Maker," 'Attar, *Manteq al-tayr,* p. 107, ll. 1932, 1936.

"Loving the Artist," 'Aisha, the daughter of Abu 'Uthman, from Nishapur. In al-Sulami, *Dhikr al-muta'abbidat al-sufiyyat.* Arabic text in Rkia E. Cornell, *Early Sufi Women,* 185. Translation modified.

"A Raging Hellfire," 'Attar, *Manteq al-tayr,* p. 110, l. 1979.

"Give It Away," 'Attar, *Manteq al-tayr,* p. 117, ll. 2098–99.

"Every Breath Is a Jewel," 'Attar, *Manteq al-tayr,* p. 126, ll. 2262–64. The last line can also be read as "you keep attaching yourself to beings other than Him."

"Idols Inside," Rumi, *Masnavi,* 1:778–79.

"What's Your Puddle of Piss?" Rumi, *Masnavi,* 1:1082–83.

"Our Brokenness," Rumi, *Masnavi,* 1:3012.

"Remove the Ka'ba," Shams-e Tabrizi, *Maqalat,* 653.

"Don't Blame the Night," Rumi, *Fihi ma fihi,* chapter 48, p. 175.

"God Remains," Fakhr al-Din 'Iraqi, *Lama'at,* chapter 26, pp. 531–32.

Index of Authors and Sources

Printed and bound by CPI Group (UK) Ltd, Croydon, CR0 4YY

02/06/2023

03223821-0001